WOMAN
in *Transition*

A catalogue record for this book is available from the British Library.

Published in the United Kingdom by Bridge Publishing.

ISBN: 978-0-9574972-0-7

WOMAN
in *Transition*

Nan McLaughlin

BRIDGE
PUBLISHING

Dedication

To my wonderful husband of 45 years, who has loved
me, supported me and encouraged me.

He is my mentor, my best friend and the one
who has always believed in me.

Thank you Bernie.

Foreword

by Dr. Beverly Womarans
Founder of CFC international

*N*an McLaughlin, author of *"Woman In Transition"* is a long time friend of mine. She is a wonderful wife, mother and grandmother, excellent speaker and pastor with a heart for women of all ages. Her book is filled with practical advice for women in all stages of life. In one chapter she touches on the importance of a single woman "being right" before looking for Mr. Right. Her chapter on divorce is filled with compassion, and good words of teaching. But best of all, she always leads the reader back to our Lord Jesus Christ and His Eternal Word. Her stories and anecdotes illustrate her points without being overwhelming.

This quick read will help women of all ages. Nan's delightful book will make a great gift for the women in your life.

Foreword

by Pastor Tom Inglis
Psalmody International
Sydney Life Christian Family Church

Women are particularly vulnerable to the onslaught of all kinds of attack and have been since the beginning of time. The enemy knows their invaluable contribution to society and will do everything to discourage them as they cope with the plethora of transitions that life inevitably brings. Everyone in todays cauldron of life faces challenges and continual transition and particularly women. They have to cope with child bearing, keeping a home, cooking, washing, and spending many hours with the children while dad is at work. In addition many women give up their dreams so they can rear a family and often deal with issues of loneliness and feelings of isolation. Additionally many divorced women feel abandoned and left to survive alone. Transition seems to be at the very core of their existence.

However this book is like a breath of fresh air to those who are gasping to know the intense love and plans God has for women. Nan introduces the reader to a loving and understanding God who is intensely interested in the fears and concerns that transition brings. She has successfully portrayed God as a loving Father who wants to help women progress through life's challenges.

Woman in Transition is a well researched guidebook for women to live as God intended, a treasure trove of insightful gems that every woman needs to know whether a teenager, mum, grandmother or business woman. Women will be encouraged as they read through the pages of this book and discover the exciting possibilities God has planned for them.

The distinguishing feature of this book is that it is not written about women, but for women. It's like a personal note to women from God, and I highly recommend that every woman irrespective of age should read it and tell others about it.

Foreword

by Lisa Bevere
Messenger International
Author/Speaker

Reading "*Woman in Transition*" is like journeying with a friend. I trust you'll be inspired and challenged by Nan. She is an amazing friend and mother in the faith.

Contents

Introduction

To women everywhere...
Don't give up. Don't look back.
You can do it. You can make it.
You are looking good.

*F*rom cradle to grave women are going to go through many times of transition. I was born in 1949, just five years after the 2nd World War. I have experienced much change in living standards and lifestyles. I have grown and changed through each season in my life. The transformation of a person is a process, not a one–time quick fix. Are you willing to enter into that process and allow God to reshape you into the woman you want to be and should be? If your answer is yes, prepare to enter the most exciting, rewarding and fulfilling time of your life. As you read and apply the principles in this book, you will experience for yourself the change you have been wanting for so long.

I have the privilege of being a minister's wife, a mother of three and at this time, grandmother to eight beautiful children. Since 1980 I have worked alongside my husband, pioneering churches in South Africa and Scotland, with a vision to reach out to the world. I have experienced the different cycles of life that women have to go through, which, as long as the earth remains, will not change. I believe in the callings and giftings of women, regardless of which career they choose to follow and I know that it is time for women to rise up and be all that they were created to be.

The women you will read about have no names, but you will identify with them. They come from different walks of lives and their issues may be your issues too. There is not a woman born into this earth who has not had to struggle with who she is and whether or not she is of value.

Abuse, low self esteem, insecurity, depression, addiction, discrimination, divorce, hormone changes and the like are just some of the issues that women have to conquer.

You may be struggling through some difficult situations in your life right now and I trust this book will give you some of the answers you are seeking. I have been open and honest as I share from my own experiences and the way I have overcome many challenges by applying the priceless principles of God's Word in my life.

The bible also contains the many mistakes that men and women of the past have made and I believe they were put there so we don't have to repeat them.

I found the solutions I needed in the bible to get me through some hard situations in my life. God gave me His word to steer me and keep me on track when I felt utterly overwhelmed and dejected. The life–giving message the bible contains transformed my life and I know it will do the same for you if you will diligently apply it trustingly.

God bless you.

Nan

Prologue

In the Garden

*H*e opened his eyes. How long had he been sleeping? Something was different. His last recollection had been of him talking with God. God saying, "You shouldn't be alone Adam". He stretched again and opened his eyes wide. He was awake now. God was walking toward him, but He was not alone. Someone walked with Him.

Adam stood up and looked with awe and wonder. He couldn't take his eyes off this beautiful creature. Strange feelings were rising up in him, different to any he had ever known. She was beautiful. He wanted to love her, cherish her, and protect her.

God spoke, "Adam, this is your completion. She was taken out from you. I shaped her and formed her". Adam called her woman because she was taken out of man.

She loved walking in the garden and drinking in the beauty and peace, which surrounded her. The flowers were vibrant with colour. The cooling water from the river was so refreshing and the fruit from the trees was so sweet and satisfying.

She was content. She was loved. She was cherished. She was protected. She had all she ever needed or desired.

She found herself in the middle of the garden and came upon the forbidden tree. What was it she had not to do, eat the fruit or touch the fruit? It didn't matter, she had been forbidden to go near it. If she did she would die. What was die?

The serpent came to her and said that God had lied to her and Adam. He said that she would not die but rather, would become very wise and that God was afraid they would be wiser than He was. What was afraid?

The tree looked good. What harm could a taste of the fruit do? "Adam, taste this fruit. It will make you wiser and you will be more like God."

As they stood together their eyes were opened and they saw their nakedness and they felt vulnerable. They were ashamed. They hid their shame from God and from one another. They heard Him call, but they were afraid. These feelings of fear and shame were new to them. They knew they had done something terrible and irrevocable.

God knew, and He cursed the serpent. He cursed the earth and banished them from the garden. From now on Adam would have to work the ground. Toil and sweat would be his portion. The woman would bear children in intense pain and suffering. One day they would face death. They knew what that was now and they were afraid.

Adam was angry with God. He blamed Him for bringing the woman to him. He blamed her for being deceived. It was all her fault! She deserved the pain and the shame.

God killed animals and covered their shame and banished them from Paradise. Adam named his wife Eve, meaning – the life giving one.

1

The Original Eve

God never created anything without purpose. First and foremost, man and woman were created to have a relationship with God.

Man was made (manufactured) out of the dust of the ground. This refers to the body, but the spirit of man was created, and woman was inside him.

It was God's intention that man should have dominion over the entire earth and all creation as we see it.

Genesis 1:26 & 27 (Amplified Bible)

God said, Let Us (Father, Son & Holy Spirit) make man in our image, after our likeness, and let them have complete authority over the fish of the sea, the birds of the air, the tame beasts, and over everything that creeps upon the earth. So God created man in His own image and likeness, male and female He created them.

God sees Adam needs a help–meet, so He puts Adam to sleep and makes (builds) woman. It was there that God separated male from female. Adam wakes up feeling a bit empty on the inside, opens his eyes, sees woman and says, "Here is my completion". He names her Woman.

Genesis 2:18–25

Now the Lord God said, It is not good that man should be alone: I will make him a help meet (suitable, adapted, complimentary) for him. And the Lord God caused a deep sleep to fall upon Adam: and while he slept, He took one of his ribs or a part of his side and closed up the place with flesh. And the rib or part of his side, which the Lord God had taken from the man, He built up and made into a woman, and He brought her to the man. Then Adam said, This creature is now bone of my bones and flesh of my flesh, she shall be called Woman because she was taken out of a man. Therefore a man shall leave his father and his mother and shall become united and cleave to his wife and they shall become one flesh. And the man and his wife were both naked and were not embarrassed or ashamed in each other's presence.

So it was in the beginning:

The perfect marriage. The perfect couple. The perfect man. The perfect woman. Having a perfect relationship in fellowship with God. They lived in perfection.

Then something happened that changed everything. The serpent beguiled the woman and she was deceived.

She in turn involved Adam in the deception and both of them disobeyed God by eating from the wrong tree!

Genesis 2:16–17 (Amplified Bible)

And the Lord God commanded the man, saying, You may freely eat of every tree in the garden. But of the tree of the knowledge of good and evil you shall not eat, for in the day you eat of it you shall surely die.

God had told them not to eat from the tree of the knowledge of good and evil. If they did, He said they would die. Up until that time there was no death, but because of their disobedience, their relationship with God was broken and man became separated from God.

As if that was not bad enough, Adam had given away the responsibility of governing the earth to Satan. He gave away his authority and dominion. Satan took Adam's authority and used it against him.

2 Corinthians 4:4 (Amplified Bible)

For the god of this world has blinded the unbeliever's minds (that they should not discern the truth) preventing them from seeing the illuminating light of the Gospel of the glory of Christ the Messiah, Who is the image and likeness of God.

Three times in the gospels Jesus called Satan the ruler of this world.

John 12:31 (New King James Version)

Now is the judgment of this world, now the ruler of this world will be cast out.

John 14:30 (New King James Version)

I will no longer talk much with you, for the ruler of this world is coming, and he has nothing in Me.

John 16:11 (New King James Version)

Of judgment, because the ruler of this world is judged.

That doesn't mean that God has lost ownership of the earth. It means that the devil is the god of this world's system. That's why the system often stinks!

Sin came into the world, the earth became cursed and no longer was everything perfect.

Romans 5:12 (New King James Version)

Therefore, just as through one man sin entered into the world, and death through sin, and thus death spread to all men, because all have sinned.

Not one person born of woman comes into this earth without bearing the stain of sin. It is because of sin that people want to blame someone. It is never their fault! The woman blamed the serpent. The man blamed the woman and God! God gets the blame for the bad stuff that happens in life, but you have to understand there was an evil force unleashed on the earth when Adam lost his dominion. Adam lost his authority and woman lost her innocence.

Genesis 3:20

The man called his wife's name Eve (life spring) because she was the mother of all the living.

All this happened at a tree, but there was another tree, many years later, where there was a great restoration for man and woman. This tree took the shape of a cross and meant that no longer would man and woman be separated from God. A man called Jesus, the Christ, died on that cross for every man and woman born into this world.

Galatians 3:13 (New King James Version)

Christ has redeemed us from the curse of the law, having become a curse for us (for it is written), cursed is everyone who hangs on a tree.

Jesus represented God here on earth. He came to redeem, which means to buy back, all that Adam had lost when he disobeyed God.

Romans 5:18 (New King James Version)

Therefore, as through one man's offence judgment came to all men, resulting in condemnation, even so through one man's righteous act the free gift came to all men, resulting in justification of life.

What Jesus did on the cross was two fold. First, He reconciled man back to God. There was now a way man could have a relationship with Him. Jesus was the mediator between you and God. Secondly, He separated man from the power of sin and the hold that Satan had over him.

1 John 3:8 (Amplified Bible)

The reason the Son of God was manifest (made visible) was to undo (destroy, loosen and dissolve) the works the devil (has done).

Basic Translation

And the Son of God was seen on earth, so that He might put an end to the works of the evil one.

Wand Translation

That He might neutralise what the devil has done.

Phillips Translation

With the express purpose of liquidating the devil's activities.

Jesus took back man's lost authority and dominion. Then He gave it back to man.

Matthew 28:18 (Amplified Bible)

All authority (all power of rule) in heaven and on earth has been given to Me.

Verse 19 *Go then...*

In other words, you can now go and represent Jesus here on earth and enforce the victory He won over Satan. As a representative of Jesus Christ, you have authority over the devil. You don't have to fear him any longer.

There are many wounded, hurting and fearful women around in this world.

She may be a woman you work beside, your next–door neighbour, or even a family member.

Her chains are alcohol, drugs, abuse, rejection, broken relationships, poverty, sickness, low self–esteem or any of the things that cause women to suffer. Many women are in that state because they don't know that Jesus liberated them at the cross.

They need someone to tell them the good news that Jesus loves them and He paid the price in full for them.

John 3:16 (Message Bible)

This is how much God loved the world. He gave His Son, His one and only Son. And this is why, so that no one need be destroyed, by believing in Him, anyone can have a whole and lasting life.

If you already know this Jesus of the cross, then you could be the one to represent Him to them. Everything that Adam and Eve lost was restored. And they lived happily ever after? I wish that was the case, but it's not. God's plan to redeem man was not flawed, but man has not understood or received this free gift of a new life in Christ. Man had to believe that Jesus was the Son of God, died on the cross and rose again from the dead on the third day.

Romans 10:8 & 9 (Amplified Bible)

But what does it say? The word (God's message in Christ) is near you, on your lips and in your heart: that is, the Word (the message) of faith, which we preach.

Because if you acknowledge and confess with your mouth that Jesus is Lord and in your heart believe (adhere to, trust in and rely on the truth) that God raised Him from the dead, you will be saved.

You too can know this Jesus of the cross. You too, can represent Him here on earth. Repent from past sins and disobedience to God, confess Jesus as your Lord and Saviour and receive forgiveness from God. Then Jesus will come and live in you, and you will become born again.

John 3:3 (Living Bible)

> *With all the earnestness I possess I tell you this: Unless you are born again, you can never get into the Kingdom of God.*

This is the Gospel message and it has everything to do with how we live in the now and where we will spend eternity.

Up until the time of Jesus, women were treated badly and many times harshly. They had no regard in the eyes of men. There was a prayer that Jewish men prayed which went something like this. "Lord God, I thank you that I am not a Gentile, a dog or a woman." To the men in those days, a woman was a possession, very much like a camel or an ox.

Every so often, a woman would shine for God, and He would cause them to do great things for Him. Like Sarah, Deborah, Ruth, Esther and others, and of course Mary, the mother of Jesus.

Jesus had a different view of women to the other men of His time, and He wanted to restore to them their self worth and purity, which woman was stripped of in Eden. He was a defender of women. He comforted them and He forgave them. We see this with the woman who was brought to him caught in the act of adultery. The men of that day wanted to stone her, but Jesus intervened and saved her life. (*John 8:3–11*)

He saved your life as well. He did this at the cross, but many women don't have the knowledge of what exactly was done for them and don't know who they are in Christ and what they have in Christ.

Although we have all we need to live an overcoming, victorious life, there is an added element involved, which Eve before she was deceived in the garden, never had to exercise. That element is faith.

Hebrews 11:1

For without faith it is impossible to please God, for he who comes to God must believe that He is and that He is a rewarder of those who diligently seek Him.

You need to believe that God has, does and will continue to love, care for, support, provide, heal, forgive, be merciful, never leave and be all in all to you.

Faith is in the heart and in the mouth. You saw that in the scripture in Romans 10 verses 8 & 9. As you read on, you will have to exercise your faith to appropriate all that God has for you and for what He wants to do in you.

Romans 12:2 (Phillips Translation)

Don't let this world shape you into its mould, But be transformed by the renewing of your mind.

God wants to conform (change) us to the image of Christ. To change our lives, we have to change our minds. Your mindset is what dictates who you are and what you accomplish, or not!

Every woman wants to be loved, appreciated, valued, honoured and treated right! Every Christian woman wants to be a good wife, mother and friend, and most importantly, be the woman God wants her to be.

You can trust God to transform you. He made you and there is only one of you. You may be fragile, but you won't break. God is great at softening you up so that He can reshape you. He knows what it takes to build a woman. He did it in the beginning and He wants to do it again in you.

As you read on through this book I believe that God will begin that reshaping process.

The women I write about are nameless. They could be you or someone you know. That does not matter. But what does matter is that you take on board the fact that you are not alone. You are not the only woman who has a past. We have all made mistakes. We all have failed at some point in our lives. We all have the same physical, emotional and spiritual issues to deal with because we are all women.

I speak to you, not as someone who has lived a perfect life. Not as someone who has never known shame. Not as someone who has never made a mistake and blown it. Not as someone who has reached perfection. I speak to you woman to woman. I will share my life's experiences and hope you will learn from them. I will share how I learned (and still am learning) to trust God and enjoy peace in my life.

Take courage. Have hope. Trust in God. You do have a destiny and it is attainable.

2

The Abused Woman

Tears were streaming down her cheeks as she turned her back on the man lying next to her. She didn't even know his name. Not that she cared who he was as she wouldn't see him again. He wasn't as rough with her as the last guy and he had told her he loved her. Deep inside she needed to hear those words. He had told her she was beautiful. That was definitely a lie! All she saw when she looked in the mirror was someone ugly and of no significance. Who would want to stay with her, take care of her? No one. Certainly not her mother and she didn't know who her father was. Ever since her mother's boyfriend had molested her when she was ten years old, she had made the decision that she was going to look after herself. No one cared. What hope had she of ever getting married and having children? Who would want her, an ugly, soiled person of bad reputation?

She was sobbing quietly now, her mind taking her down roads she didn't want to go. She tried to imagine herself as a princess who marries her prince and lives happily ever after. Reality set in when the man next to her turned around and began to fondle her. She slapped him and told him to go back to sleep. He slapped her back... Hard!

Afterwards, when she knew he was sleeping soundly, she got up and went to the kitchen in the shabby bed-sit. Where had she put the pills? Happy pills she called them. She always took double the prescribed dose and that put her to sleep. Sleep meant forgetfulness and sometimes, wonderful dreams.

What would happen if she took the whole bottle of pills? Then she wouldn't have to wake up and face another day and night. No one would miss her. No one cared. No one would ever love her. Her mother had told her she was to blame for everything. Her father would still have been around if her mother hadn't got pregnant with her. She was never meant to be. She was unloved and unwanted. An accident.

Her mother was right! She was a bad person. She deserved to be abused. She deserved to be punished!

She had heard once that God loved everyone and sent His son Jesus to die on the cross so that their sins could be forgiven. Her mind took her back to that day. It was summer and there was a church holding an open-air gospel crusade in the town. She had run from the house that day to get away from her mother's boyfriend. She had liked the singing and the clapping and had listened as the man had shared about how God loved everyone.

He had pointed at her and said, "He loves you pet and He will look after you." Well, if there was a God, He hadn't done much of a job, had He? People had prayed that day to 'get saved' whatever that was! No, she didn't think God loved her. No one did. After all, wasn't it woman that was to blame for sin in the first place? That's what she was taught at school in religious education.

Why had her mother called her Eve? She felt responsible for all the rubbish in the world because her name was Eve. Even the name, to her, represented shame, sin, and deception. The first Eve was a bad person and so was she. So there it was.

Her mind took her back to the bottle of pills. What was it she was going to do? Sleep… that was it. She needed to forget. She would only take a couple of pills tonight.

Tomorrow she would go and see the new lady doctor. She had been kind and had listened to her. "You are a lovely young woman with your whole life ahead of you. You can change" she had said. She had cried, not because she was afraid of change but because of the kindness and concern she had seen in her eyes. The same kindness and concern she had seen in the eyes of the minister that day at the gospel meeting, "God loves you pet", he had said.

Could someone really love her? Perhaps she could change…

Even if the original Eve made a mess, God could clean her up and change her. Maybe there was hope for her.

3

Overcoming Abuse

Self Worth

Women who have been abused and mistreated have no self worth and feel they have no significance. Usually they have been stripped of all their dignity and femininity. They are used as sex objects and punching bags for men to vent their anger, frustration and lust on. Many times they have been verbally abused by the people closest to them. Verbal abuse can leave scars which many women carry throughout their lives. Words have the power to create life or death.

> **Proverbs 18:21 (Amplified Bible)**
>
> *Death and life are in the power of the tongue, and they who indulge in it shall eat the fruit of it, for death or life.*

These women live with fear and do not have any kind of normality in their lives. Just to survive from day to day is all they can cope with. This becomes even more difficult, if they have children living with them. For them to trust in a man again is nigh on impossible, but nothing is impossible with God.

Every woman derives her self worth from the men in her life. This begins with her father, brothers, boyfriends, and ultimately, her husband. If a woman does not get that affirmation, she will look elsewhere for it, and that is where many women get themselves into wrong and abusive relationships.

It is so important for fathers to affirm their daughters. My daughter was born in 1974 and has three children, but my husband still sits her on his knee and tells her how special she is and how good she is doing as a wife and mother.

Husbands need to tell their wives they are loved and appreciated even when they get it wrong. Women need to know that they are not a disappointment.

Every woman wants to be cherished, loved, protected, provided for and taken care of by the man in her life. Abused women have never known that and think wrongly, that their lives can never change or get better. Many of them drift from one abusive relationship into another.

Why is this? I believe this happens because the woman believes she deserves the punishment and she then submits to the abuse in whatever form that takes.

When a woman decides enough is enough and stops submitting to the abuse, she breaks free from whatever was holding her in that trap.

Most times women need someone to show them they can change and that they deserve better. They need someone to walk them through the change process and support them while they go through that. Don't sit around waiting for change to strike! You need to choose to change. You need to follow through with your decision to change and get the help you need to do it. But before you can have change in your life, something has to die. Before you birth something new there needs to be a funeral. Funerals bring closure to the past. You need to let go of the past to lay hold of the future. This is the essence of change. People don't resist change but they do resist loss. The familiar, even if it is hard, is sometimes all they know. Change means embracing new thought processes and requires a step of faith to implement it.

Romans 6:11

Consider yourself dead to harmful behaviours in your life.

John 12:24

Unless a grain of wheat falls into the earth and dies it will not produce.

You need to die to the old responses and feelings of low self esteem in your life and get a new mindset that affirms your value and self worth in God's eyes and in your own estimation. You need to embrace the fact that you are worth something and you are not somebody's dog's body to be abused, cursed or ignored.

There are many reasons why people desire to change. It can be a triggering event, like the death of a loved one, a job lost, a business failed or a crisis situation. Maybe you have reached your limit and have decided enough is enough. If you are in an abusive situation, you need your circumstances to change for your own safety and for the safety of any children you may have or are yet to have. Regardless of the reason for change, you need to understand the process of change. You need to deal with the influences of your past. Say goodbye to the ghosts of the past and move on without any baggage.

Just as you can't drive a car by looking in the rear view mirror, so you can't go forward in life always looking back to the past.

Philippians 3:13 (Amplified Bible)

I do not consider brethren that I have captured and made it my own yet: but one thing I do (it is my one aspiration) forgetting what lies behind and straining forward to what lies ahead.

(Message Bible)

Friends, don't get me wrong. By no means do I count myself an expert in all of this, but I've got my eye on the goal, where God is beckoning us onward – to Jesus. I'm off and running, and I'm not turning back.

Break all hindering and fruitless associations. Get around the right people. You will either increase or decrease through your associations. Ask yourself this question. Do my friends add to my life or do they subtract from my life? Identify and free yourself from all your limiting assumptions and hindering beliefs. You can change your life by changing your mind. Your mind is made up of thoughts, feelings and beliefs. This in turn affects your behaviour, which determines the results you have in your life.

Sow a thought, reap an action. Sow an action, reap a habit. Sow a habit, reap a lifestyle.

Don't allow hindering beliefs about yourself. There is no shortcut to change and it helps when you understand what the process is.

1. You decide to change.
2. Remember that every change begins with an ending!
3. You have to move on.
4. You may even experience a sense of loss as you walk away from the old ways and lifestyle but have the funeral, and get closure.
5. Don't wallow in the loss. Yes, you were wronged and no, you didn't deserve all the stuff you went through, but don't drift back into your comfort zone or get into denial. Face the facts and push through.
6. When all your negative emotions start to kick in; fear, guilt, grief, depression and self–loathing, don't get angry with God and say "Why me?" What you are going through is part of the change process, so don't resist the change but work through the negative emotions.
7. Don't let pride stop you from asking for the help and support you need.

You know you are through the worst, when you can look back on the past and reflect on the things that were not good, without all the negative emotions overwhelming you. You may even look back and be able to remember some of the good times with fondness.

You are now ready to embrace your new life and commit to new relationships. You can now set long–term goals and have a vision for the future. You have hope once more and you can develop a trust and confidence in the God of the second chance.

Just as the original Eve had an intimate relationship with God in the garden, so too can every woman. The first step is asking God to take control of your life and inviting Jesus into your heart. From there begins a wonderful partnership into a love relationship, which is very intimate. Thoughts and desires are shared; struggles and fears are brought into the open and swallowed up by faith and confident trust in the person of Father God. He speaks to us, in and through the scriptures in the Bible.

God can do what doctors and social workers cannot do. He can do surgery on your heart and put you back together again. Deliver the ownership of your life to God and let Him help you.

Proverbs 3:5–6 (Amplified Bible)

Trust in the Lord with all your heart and lean not, do not rely on your own understanding. In all your ways, know, recognise and acknowledge Him, and He will direct and make straight and plain your paths.

Because His Spirit lives in us and we are able to understand what the scriptures are saying, we can learn His characteristics, which are:

*   He loves us.

*   He won't let us down.

*   He protects us.

*   He provides for us.

*   He heals and restores us.

*   He is merciful and forgiving towards us.

*   He will never leave us nor forsake us.

If woman is to be the completion of man, she first needs to be complete in herself. This can only happen when she has that relationship with a God who is all these things to her. She then won't have to depend on the affirmation of the men around her, but she will be affirmed and confident of her value as a woman and assured that she is much loved. Only complete in that knowledge, can she then stand beside her husband, facing the challenges of life and building her marriage to ensure family stability and purpose.

Apart from daily communication with our Father God, there is no way woman can be transformed. Change begins in our spirit, the very core of our being. We have to allow God's hand to run over us, cutting, moulding and reshaping. When we read scriptures that speak to us concerning those things we need to change or lay down – that is the cutting.

Hebrews 4:12 (Amplified Bible)

For the word that God speaks is alive and full of power (making it active, operative, energising and effective) it is sharper than any two edged sword, penetrating to the dividing line of the breath of life (soul) and (the immortal) spirit, and of the joints and marrow (of the deepest part of our nature) exposing and sifting and analysing and judging the very thoughts and purposes of the heart.

The word working in this way is described as a two edged sword. When the word or the Spirit of God speaks to our hearts about God's love for us, it brings healing and affirmation – this is the moulding and reshaping. Hardened hearts become soft and pliable. Pride is laid down and humility rises up. Instead of resisting God's advances, we resist ungodly urges and temptations. Like a princess bride, we look forward to those times alone with our Prince and our desires become one with His.

The reshaping process has begun and we are infused with new hope, new life, new energy, which is born in our spirits and emanates our very being. People begin to notice the change.

I challenge you to make the decision to change today. Consider your current circumstances and ask yourself if this is God's best for you. When you choose to change, you choose to grow.

4

The Rebellious Teenager

The man on the bus was staring at her legs again. The skirt was even shorter when she sat down. She didn't like the look of him. She stared him down and gave him one of her "I've got power over men" looks. "Look all you like mister, but that's all you can do." She secretly liked it when she got men's attention. She didn't understand she was messing with danger.

She wished she could be popular, like the pop idols and film stars she read about in the tabloids. She wanted people chasing after her so they could take her photo. She wanted to do what she liked, eat what she wanted to eat, and dress like she wanted to dress, in comfortable jeans and a t–shirt. When you are famous, you can wear what you want, but to be accepted, you have to conform. The short skirt and skimpy top she had on were so uncomfortable, but it was what all the girls were wearing. She would never dare to be different, because that meant defying the peer pressure from her friends. As it was, she was defying her parents.

If they saw what she was wearing, they would be furious. She had a row with her Mum about what she was wearing and had stomped out the house shouting at her. She hated her Mum!

She got off the bus, but didn't head for school. She had arranged to meet some of the 'cool' girls at the café for a smoke and hot chocolate. They would have to watch out for the truant officer. If their parents found out they had bunked school they would all be in big trouble. What could her parents do anyhow? If they tried anything she would call 'Child line". It had worked the last time she threatened them with that. Funnily enough, it didn't make her feel good.

Her 'friends' were talking about the usual; boys, clothes, money and how rubbish their parents and teachers were. They had made a pact to leave school as soon as it was legal. They knew all they needed to know and school was boring. She didn't think it was. In fact, she actually liked school, but it wasn't cool to show academic interest or to excel in any way, so she put on a front of boredom and superiority. Wasn't she in the 'in group'? Wasn't she part of the intimidation and disruption in the classroom?

They had decided to hang out at one of the guy's homes tonight. His parents were away for the weekend and she would tell her parents that she was spending the night with her girlfriend. They were stupid enough to believe anything after all. She would smoke some hash and have a couple of those nice, fruity Alco pop drinks. Mixed with the hash, she got drunk quickly.

She had better make sure she had condoms at the ready. She pushed the guilt down. All her friends had sex and slept around. Remaining a virgin these days was archaic.

Why wait till she got married? She wasn't getting pregnant, and had not met anyone she felt she wanted to share the rest of her life with, so she might as well 'try' different boys. She was enjoying herself. Yet why was she crying more and more lately? Why did she feel empty, dirty and used? A hard case, her Mum had called her, unthankful. Wasn't it her right to have everything provided for her? So what if her parents were in debt? She wasn't going to be seen wearing cheap gear with no designer label on it.

Her face was heavy with make up and her hair–streaked red and purple. On Monday at school, some youth from one of the local churches had come and entertained them with some music and drama at assembly. Her friends had sneered at them, but secretly she had been moved by their sincerity and faith in God. They seemed to have fun and were so close to each other. She had long since lost the power to have fun, but had become good at pretending. She knew she had lost something precious in her life. She was missing out on something wonderful! But, she didn't know what it was. Was it perhaps the power to make choices and not be led by peer pressure? Could it be that these young people held the answer? Could she dare to be different? Fresh and clean, not stale and dirty. Open and honest, not sullen and deceitful. Being a caring person and not rebellious and defiant.

Was it too late for her? They had said it wasn't. They had said that if you were sincerely sorry for your wrong doing, and asked God to forgive you, He would. And He would give you a clean slate with a fresh start. It would be like she was born again. Yes. That's what they called it. Being born again. You couldn't earn it. You just had to receive it. Could she let the real person inside her out and for once, follow her true instincts on the inside and do what she knew to be right? Yes, she could, and she would try. She had never prayed before and she didn't know how, but she managed to get the words out. "I'm sorry God for all the bad stuff I've done and for all the lies I've told my Mum. I want that Jesus those kids were talking about, to come into my life and give me a new start." She was crying, but it was a good crying! Every tear she shed seemed to clean her up. All the guilt and shame began to lift and she felt at peace for the first time in her life.

She got home that evening having decided not to go to her friend's house. Her Mum was in the kitchen making the dinner. She saw that the ironing had been done and needed to be put away. She had never helped her mum before, even when she knew she came home tired after working in the checkout till at the supermarket. She had been so selfish. A love for her Mum rose up in her and she started crying again. She went to her room and changed into her comfortable jeans and a t–shirt. She removed the heavy makeup and brushed the spikes out of her hair. She had lovely hair under all the purple and red colouring. She took the ring out of her lip. She had gone through so much pain getting her lip pierced and for what?

She put the ironing away and sat down at the table. Her Mum came through from the kitchen and she saw how sad and weary she looked. She had never noticed that before. She knew she was responsible for the sadness, but she was going to change that. She was a new person. The old person was gone and the new person was about to give her Mum a hug and tell her she was sorry for all the pain and heartache she had caused.

An excitement and a joy rose up in her. The possibilities were unlimited. She could do something worthwhile with her life. She had purpose. She had hope. But most of all, she had God and He was on her side. He would help her. She would go down to that church tonight and speak to someone there. It may be that they could help her. She knew she had a lot to learn, but she had time on her side.

After all, fourteen wasn't old.

5

Parenting Your Teenager

*B*ringing up children is hard work! We have the God given task of teaching and training our children and hopefully they will become responsible adults so they can take their place in life. But, between the cute baby stage and the end product, we are faced with the teenager stage! It is usually in the puberty stages that children go through what can be a difficult time and parents sometimes find it hard to cope with the mood swings and the constant changes they see in their child.

I remember the challenges we faced with our two sons and our daughter. Thankfully, they got through their teen years without too much turmoil, but we did have to make adjustments. I prayed for them daily. This is very important. We must commit our children to God on a daily basis. They face so many temptations nowadays. The media is throwing everything across their path – sex, drugs, pornography, humanism, Satanism and more – so you need to cover your child with prayer.

PRAY

I pray every day for my family and I cover them with the blood of Jesus Christ. I pray *Psalm 91* over them. I encourage you to read this psalm and write it down and make it part of your prayer over your family. When we pray God's word, we pray God's will.

SET BOUNDARIES

Don't be afraid to lay down boundaries. They are what bring security.

Be clear. Be consistent. Be fair. Be flexible.

There is a difference between flexibility and compromise. Learn to listen to your child, before you tell them no. There are times when you have to trust your child to do the right thing and commit them to God's care. You can do that without compromising the truth in God's word.

I love to be with young people. I enjoy their company and whenever I can, I give them positive input and encouragement. Ask yourself the question: What is it that influences your children? Is it music? TV? DVD's? Games? Friends? Peer pressure? Parents, we must have open communication with them and give them positive input. We blew it as parents many times, but we learnt from our mistakes!

Don't let your teenager intimidate you or manipulate you. If you do, you are in for a life of misery. They will come up with stuff that is meant to get you to compromise what you know to be right. Don't do it. Stick to the boundaries you have set down for them and be consistent. The rewards are worth it.

The reason many teens lose respect for their parents, is because they see them change their minds and procrastinate when it comes to making decisions. You may not be a strong person in yourself, but you are a strong person in the Lord and in the power of His might. When I felt myself weaken and was ready to give into my teenager's unrealistic demands, I would take time out and pray. That would make the world of difference. They knew that if I got to praying, there would be no changing my mind or the outcome. The answer remained "No!" I remember the day our oldest son came to his father to ask him if he could get his ears pierced so he could wear an earring!

Now the culture here in the UK is very pro earrings & tattoos, but we lived in South Africa at that time and it was definitely not the thing to do! Our son had made some very 'cool' friends who liked to be up to speed with the latest European fashion. He was getting a lot of attention from the girls, which kind of went to his head. I will never forget my husband's answer to the earring question. "You get an earring and I'll cut your ear off while you are sleeping!" He just looked at his Dad, looked at me, and saw there was going to be no room for negotiation. We can laugh now and see the funny side, but at the time he was not a happy laddie! He later got his qualifications in engineering and was very much into rugby and sports and was so thankful he never went ahead with the earring.

We see so many young men and women here in Scotland, with tattoos and piercing in all kinds of body parts! We don't make it an issue as we are thankful that they come to church and tattoos or not, God loves them. Many of them regret their impulsiveness and some even pay a lot of money to have the tattoos removed. When it comes to job interviews and responsible positions, many employers are not into that kind of expression in young people. I use that wording kindly.

I am by no means a 'fuddy duddy' (otherwise known as an old grouch). We have to understand that the youth culture in the church today has changed so much. The surfing culture and influence is very much a part of the status quo, and we must not get into legalism when it comes to how young people dress. As long as they are covering what needs to be covered and they are not baring a lot of flesh, then we need not get on their case. God looks on their heart and I can tell you they have a heart to worship. I just love the music and lyrics that are being produced by young men and women from all over the world. I love their style and their genuine faith in God. They are not ashamed of the gospel of Christ and express their love for God through their music. If we really believe we are the church of the future, then we better get with it and open wide our church doors to the youth.

We have a lot of young people in our youth who come in with all sorts of weird and wonderful things, and every one of them are loved and accepted for who they are. It would not be pleasing to God for us to set ourselves up as critics and judges of people just because they are different, especially our young men and women.

However, I do believe that as a mother, you can pass on wisdom when it comes to these things. Remind your son or daughter that one day, they may regret it, and ask them to really consider the implications. It would seem that in my case, our eldest son was the pioneer of the hard questions! When he was sixteen, he wanted a motorbike, but at that time in South Africa, the fatalities were very high in motorbike accidents. He pushed, he moaned, he threatened, he entreated, he bribed, he even helped in the house, but sadly for him, it was all for naught. My husband and I were in total agreement – no motorbike. Most of his friends had bikes, but some of them had already been involved in accidents, one even fatally. I mentioned earlier that there are times you can be flexible. At that time we lived in a small town in the country and there were loads of wide–open spaces for scrambling and off –road bikes. My husband took him to the motorbike shop and bought him a brand new Honda 500cc off–road bike. It was a beauty. He was to share it with his brother and of course, my husband. (Who, by the way, was also into motorbikes when he was a teenager.)

Those boys got so much enjoyment out of that bike and although they had some scrapes, they were much safer than being on a road bike. My husband did manage to come off it a good few times, but for fear of retribution I won't go into that! Our son never asked us again for a road bike and when he reached his seventeenth birthday, he sat his driving test, passed, and then asked me for the keys of my beloved, blue, Volkswagen Beetle.

Then proceeded to drive it, into a wall! That is another story, a very sad one for the car and for me! But since love covers all, and I love my son, I won't go into that, for now, but I can be bought son, if you're reading this book... For the record, he is married to a wonderful woman and has two children. He did get his road bike eventually and I sometimes look after the children to let him and his wife have time out on the bike. He is part of our Christian motorcycle group at our church 'The Bridge Bikers!' Times change!

So there are times you can and should bend a bit. You can break a child's spirit by being totally inflexible. When in doubt, pray, and then follow after peace. And never ever compromise God's Word, whether the written word, or the direction of the Holy Spirit.

Did that mean that I never got it wrong? No. There were times I did the wrong thing and said the wrong thing and believe me, those teens will remember everything you said and will hold it against you! When that happened, I would throw myself on their mercy and cry "Grace" to the mountain! That would get them laughing and in agreement with my decision. You see, I learned quickly that teenagers are inherently selfish. They think the whole world revolves around them. It's all about their thoughts, their feelings, their space, their ideas, etc, etc, etc.

Only by cultivating open and honest communication with them, can you input into their lives and influence their selfish way of thinking into becoming unselfish.

A GOOD LOCAL CHURCH

Your teens need to attend a good, solid church with a vibrant youth ministry. Our daughter & son–in–law are the youth ministers in our church. They really love and care for the teenagers and they are constantly communicating that to them. The teens love and respect them, and this may come as a surprise to you, but they really appreciate the boundaries and respect codes that they have to comply with. They are learning to be accountable and responsible. They are learning to get their hormones under control and not feel they have to prove their sexuality to one another. You should see what happens to the guys when the girls come on the scene, and visa versa! One of the boundaries set at youth is No Snogging! (aka sucking face or kissing!) This is a biggie for teens.

Ninety five percent of the youth that come to our church have unsaved parents, who are totally disinterested in God and church. Some of them actually discourage their children from coming to the youth service and would be happier if their son or daughter were down in the clubs drinking and all the stuff that 'normal' children do! I had a mother say to me once that she was concerned for her daughter who had started attending church and was reading a bible. The mother's reaction to this was that she would rather her daughter went out with her friends clubbing, as it wasn't natural for a young girl not to do that! We thank God for our young people and we can see great change in them, as they begin to apply God's word in their lives and get involved in church.

But we have to cover them in prayer constantly. We can't rely on their parents getting them to do God's will, or teaching them the things of God. We do, of course, also pray for the parents and have seen a few of them become Christians and start coming to church as well, especially when they see the positive change in their children.

I believe our youth will be the first generation Christians in families and that they will be the ones to lead their parents and family to God.

We are already experiencing this in our church and have seen four generations of one family coming to God. As pastors of a church, my husband and I invest heavily into our children and youth ministries. They are not only the church of the future, but very much the church of today.

I know we will see great increase as we continue to sow into their lives, but we do have a lot of issues we have to deal with here in Scotland, that are not usual in other cultures.

One of the biggest challenges our youth face is binge drinking. With the sale of cheap alcohol and the fruity Alco pops, younger children are getting involved in drinking. It has become so bad in our area, that the government are finally trying to do something about it, but it is a case of too little, too late! We are reaching out to these children with a positive message of love and acceptance and believe that we can turn things around, one child at a time.

We encourage the youth to persevere with their education and not to drop out of school. The statistics for young people dropping out of education here in Scotland is alarming. But that is changing in our area because of the positive input they are receiving. They are also encouraged to get involved in sports and music. We continue to do whatever we can to help them.

We recently showed the teaching series 'Purity's Power' by Lisa Bevere, to the girls in our church. This had a positive effect on them and made a difference to how they saw themselves and to their confidence. Teenage pregnancy is on the increase in the UK and has become a real issue, which needs to be tackled. Providing contraception is not solving the problem of unwanted pregnancies. The morning after pill is now legally available here without parental consent for girls as young as fourteen. Abortions are also readily available. Cervical cancer is on the increase because of sexually transmitted diseases. What is the answer for these young women? How can you, as a mother, make a difference?

Well, you can begin in your home. Do you know what social networks your child is involved with? Have you checked out their Facebook, My Space, Twitter, Bebo, or whatever page of theirs? You can learn a lot by doing this and you will also be able to see who their friends are. This in turn will give you insight into the influences they are exposed to. Their behaviour, whether good or bad, is a result of the influences around them. Your job is to encourage the good influences and discourage the negative ones.

This is not rocket science but just good common sense. If you influence your teenagers, they in turn will influence their friends. As women, we have to start somewhere and our own home should be our first priority. Don't get so involved in trying to solve the world's problems, that you are ignoring the ones right under your nose!

Again, you need to pray for your children. Ask God for Godly friends for them. Pray for Godly spouses for them. Communicate with them. Know their friends and their friends' parents. Be interested in what are the important years in their lives. Praise them often. Be loving, but firm.

Don't give up on your teenager. Commit he or she to God and cast all your cares on Him.

1 Peter 1:7 (Amplified Bible)

Casting the whole of your care (all your anxieties, all your worries, all your concerns, once and for all) on Him for He cares for you affectionately and cares about you watchfully.

Don't you think that He can care for your child better than you can? Don't you know that He knows the end from the beginning? When you are lying awake at night worrying about your child, you have not truly cast your care on God.

If you need help and advice and you are part of a good, strong local church, you can get the help you need there. We have a great support system in the church and many of the parents regularly get together and share with one another. This helps put things into perspective. You may find that you are not the only parent working through a certain situation. You may also begin to count your blessings when you hear what some parents are working through!

If you are not hooked into a good church, I strongly advise you to find one as soon as you can. Make sure it is a bible-based, family church with a strong children's and youth ministry. Many times children drift away from God because they are in churches which are not relevant to them and do not cater for teens.

I pray that God will give you wisdom, strength and help, as you guide your teenager through these very important years of their lives.

6

The Single Woman

She walked into her empty flat. She felt the cold after being in her warm car for the one-hour drive it took her to get home from work.

Home!

This wasn't a home. It was a place to sleep. She hardly ever cooked a meal for herself. The new kitchen she had put in was a waste of time and money, but it would add value to the property. Buying the flat had been a good move, as it was already worth a good bit more than she had paid for it four years earlier. She had bought the flat when she was twenty-seven. She had thought that by this time she would have been married and had started a family. She didn't want to think about that or she would get depressed. She felt that time was running out for her.

She hadn't met anyone yet who flicked her switch, but at this stage she would settle for companionship. She felt overwhelmed at times with loneliness.

She could not go on this way, night after night, and day after day.

There was no mail for her and no messages on the answer phone. She still lived in hope though and checked her messages whenever she got in the door. The radio was still on from the morning. She liked having some background noise as she found silence disconcerting. Her friend had asked her to go to the movies with her but she couldn't be bothered. She was tired when she got home from work, and didn't feel like getting dressed up to go out.

She must have fallen asleep watching TV. It was dark outside and the heating had gone off, so she knew it must be after eleven. It was 1am. It wasn't worth going to her bed now. Her alarm would go off in a few hours time. She pulled the throw over her and went back to sleep. Tomorrow's another day. Maybe she would meet Mr Right and live happily ever after. Yes, in her dreams!

She awoke to the buzzing of the alarm. The sun was shining brightly, the birds were singing and she felt good and rested. She didn't realise she had been so tired. Her job was stressful at times, but nothing she couldn't cope with.

When she got into work, there was a pile of files on her desk, which she had to work through. Slowly and methodically, she dealt with them one by one, and managed to clear her desk just before stopping time.

It was Friday and she always went out with the girls for a coffee on Friday nights. She looked forward to this, it being the highlight of her social week. Now that was sad! She always took more care with her appearance on Fridays. After all, she never knew whom she might meet. Just maybe!

The café was packed and they found themselves squeezed into a corner with a mass of bodies pressing in against them. Café culture had spread and it was the in thing to do. Many people were foregoing meeting in the pubs, preferring the atmosphere in the cafés. She sipped her latte and enjoyed spooning the froth into her mouth. She wasn't aware that she had a frothy moustache until the guy sitting across from her indicated by rubbing his finger over his top lip. When she cottoned on to his meaning, she was embarrassed and her face went red. He leaned over to her and apologised. "Didn't mean to embarrass you, but I didn't think you would like to go around with a milky top lip all night". She thanked him and looked away.

He was nice looking and had an open face. He started talking to her and she found herself laughing and enjoying his company. He was so easy to talk to. There was none of the awkwardness she usually experienced when she met guys for the first time.

She was just about to ask him where he worked when a lovely looking blonde woman walked up and put her arms round his neck. He turned round and smiled up at her. "I was wondering when you were going to turn up. Come and meet..." He went quiet. Where was the young woman he had been talking to? Oh well, she probably had to leave.

She was crying softly in the toilet. She had set herself up for disappointment yet again. How many times must she put herself through this? It seemed like all the guys she liked were already taken! Was there no hope for her? Was she destined to live her life out as an old, dried out spinster?

'You OK?" It was one for her friends looking for her. "I'm fine". She pulled herself together and joined her friends. The guy she had been talking to was now gazing into the eyes of the attractive blonde. When he saw her watching him, he waved. "There you are. I thought you had left. Let me introduce you to my sister Lucy". His sister Lucy! There was a God in heaven after all. She smiled and started chatting to Lucy. She was also so easy to get on with and would make a wonderful sister in law!

"You have a lovely smile you know" he said. "Would you like to join us for a movie and some Italian afterwards?"

Would I just!

7

Preparing for Marriage

Song of Solomon 2:7

Do not awaken love before its time.

There are a lot of single women in our church, ranging from teens to mature women and for all, the above statement is true. Don't bend to peer pressure, but wait for the right man to come along. As women, we need to set our standards to God's standards.

Many women are in love with love! This is what I call stupid devotion. Don't put your life on hold, waiting for love. The important thing is not finding the right person, but being the right person. Once you 'be' the right person, you are then ready for the right person to come and share their life with you. When you are complete in Christ, you are so much more able to make the correct choices when it comes to relationships and that can save you a lot of grief.

So many young women are struggling with loneliness. They want a husband and children, and feel that they have "missed the boat" if they haven't done that by the time they are thirty. People are marrying later in life than they did years ago and many couples just don't want to get married, for fear of commitment. I believe this fear is mainly with men, because they don't want to take their responsibility as husbands or fathers. This attitude is very prevalent in our society today, and women and children suffer because of it.

My husband has a real desire to see men take their place as men and not be afraid to face the future as a husband and father. We live in a fatherless world, and we can see the negative results of this all around us. Being a male is a matter of birth, but being a man is a matter of choice. These are the words of Dr Ed Cole from his acclaimed book, Maximised Manhood. Children grow up not knowing what it's like to have both parents at home and have no idea of what a stable family life should be. The world around us is so out of order that normal now includes all sort of different connotations when it comes to family.

Many couples live together outside of marriage and go from one relationship to another, without any thought of the damage they are doing to their children. Young girls get pregnant and without the support of their family, they and their children are vulnerable to the deceptions of men looking for easy sex. Often these girls have children to different fathers, who never commit or take responsibility for them.

Through divorce, or partnership breakdowns, there can be children from different partners all living in the same home, hence the term, blended families. In our church we have many families who fall into this category, but thank God, they are stable, and with God at the centre of their lives, have made the necessary adjustments, so that the children have a secure and happy home.

Every woman wants a husband who will provide stability and security, and who is committed to her for the duration and not only when it suits him.

I have watched women throw away all their standards and their reputation just so they could get a partner and not be alone. Most of them live to regret it.

As a woman, this is what you should be looking for in a man:

* A man who believes in God and is serving God consistently
* A man who keeps his word. His yes should always mean yes
* A man who is loving by nature
* A man of prayer
* A man who is a leader
* A man who is a good provider by working and holding down a job
* A man who praises you for the person you are.

When you find a man who has these characteristics, marry him!

There was a young, single lady in our church who wanted to get married and have children, but was content to wait till the right man came along. She was not anxious at all and quite at peace with her singleness. On talking to her, she shared that she was using the time she had to prepare herself for her husband. She would read books on how to pray for your husband, how to be a good wife etc. She knew exactly what she was looking for in a husband, and wanted to make sure that she had all the qualities a man is looking for in a woman. That young woman is now married to a wonderful Christian man who loves her and cares for her. She is so glad she waited for the right man and did not get involved in wrong relationships. She is in fact, married to our son! We are so thankful for her and she and our son are very happy together.

What are these qualities men are looking for, you might ask?

The word wife means helpmeet. A wife is to be a support to her husband. She is to under gird and help him. She is to hold up her man and be the hidden spring of his life. She needs to be a spiritually strong woman, whose mouth is filled with kindness. There are many women whose tongues are full of poison by constantly moaning and complaining. Do you think any man is going to want to get involved with someone like that? I think not. Men are looking for homemakers, not home breakers! If you, as a single woman, are not skilled in any of these areas, then you need to start learning. You don't want to wait till the right man comes along and you realise you don't know the first thing about homemaking, cooking, children and all the areas that come under the responsibility of being a wife.

As a young wife, I did not have a clue how to cook. I could clean house, as I used to help my Mum at home. I could bake wee sponge cakes because I learned that at school. But, my young, hard working husband needed more than fairy cakes when he came home from a hard day's work! I had to learn fast how to prepare reasonably good meals. You don't need to be like me and be unprepared. Get yourself some cookery books or watch one of the many cookery programmes on TV. It can be fun trying out new recipes. But try them out on your close friends first! They will tell you the truth and won't sue you for food poisoning!!

Proverbs 31:10

A virtuous woman who can find? Her price is far above rubies or pearls.

The woman in *Proverbs 31* was a composite of many women; otherwise she would have to be superwoman! She was a successful mother. She feared the Lord. She had self-esteem and value. She is special and she has worth. Her price is far above rubies.

When it comes to marriage, women literally have to sleep in the bed they make for themselves!

I understand that it can be difficult at times, when you see your friends getting married and having children, while you are still waiting for your husband to come along. It is during these times, that you have to ask God to help you through them, and to allow His strength to lift you up and cover the loneliness. You have to take authority over any thought processes that get you thinking you are ugly, unmarriageable, unworthy or any other thing that causes you to feel bad about yourself. Don't allow your mind to take you down the road of pity parties, or feelings of rejection etc, etc, etc, etc! God is the original matchmaker and you need to trust Him to hook you up with the right man for you.

How will He do this?

The same way He does everything else in our lives – by divine appointments and connections. If you never go out and show yourself friendly, how are you ever going to meet people? You need to have friends from all different aspects of life. Don't just stay around single people. Married couples have family and friends that are single too! You just may be the ideal woman for their single brother or cousin!

Be at peace and wait. Don't lose hope and don't drop your standards. Trust God in all your ways and He will direct your steps. He knows the end from the beginning. You can't see the big picture, but God can. Don't limit God and don't limit yourself. Be open to new friendships and watch and see what the Lord will do.

Don't be tempted to get into a physical relationship with a man because your hormones are working overtime! You hope he will still love you! The lines of an old song come to mind.

Tonight you're mine completely,

You gave your love so sweetly

Tonight, the light of love is in your eyes,

Will you still love me tomorrow?

The answer is NO!!

They say you don't truly know somebody until you live with them – so for those who are thinking about giving "living together" a try first before deciding to marry, DON'T! Yes, he may still love you in the morning and if by God's grace you do end up getting married, you will have achieved the end result, but I believe God has a much better plan for you. If he doesn't value you enough to marry you first, he doesn't deserve you, and if you go down that route, you may be entering a lifetime of regrets and misery. Don't risk your whole future by making bad choices.

Thank God there is forgiveness, but when the man God has chosen for you does come along, you will regret the fact that you don't come to him as a virgin. You need to nurture a godly character and not compromise! Don't do anything that you would not be comfortable doing if your parents were with you! Cheap lust can never be compared to love and healthy desire.

Be aware of the signals that you give to men by the way that you dress and look. Men want to protect and provide for women. Bring that out in your man. The "power woman", and the "independent woman" brings out the worst in men, who then want to dominate, dictate and control.

If you have been sexually active, it is still not too late to change. If we ask God to forgive us, He will, and He cleanses us, but you have to forgive yourself and start afresh. Keep yourself for your husband. Step out of the shadows of sin into a new future. You are forgiven, so go and sin no more.

Surrender your relationships to God and ask for His help and intervention. Remember, man cannot fill the emptiness inside you. Only God can do that if you will pursue Him and rely on Him. Are you strong enough to give up control of your life and embrace the great future God has for you?

Jeremiah 29:11 (Amplified Bible)

For I know the thoughts and plans I have for you, says the Lord, thoughts and plans for welfare and peace and not for evil, to give you hope in your final outcome.

God is concerned for you and your future and I pray you will surrender your will to His will and let Him guide you and lead you in the way that you should go. Your destiny and your husband await you. I believe God is saying to you, "Be at peace and fret not, but surrender your life to Me, and allow Me to lead you and guide you in all your ways."

May you know God's love and comfort and never feel alone again.

8

Denise's Story

We returned to Scotland from South Africa when our daughter was thirteen. She had to go to a new high school, where she did not know anyone and where the teaching methods used were so different. It was a total culture shock for her. She had been part of a vibrant youth group at our church in South Africa, and since we were pioneering our first church in Scotland, there was no youth ministry in the church. It would be an understatement to say that it was a difficult time for her and our two sons.

We knew that God had called us back to Scotland, so we prayed and asked Him to intervene on our children's behalf. Denise did fairly well at school and got her higher certificates in secretarial studies. She left school and got a training position in the local council offices. There weren't many Christians around and since she didn't go to discos or clubs she found it hard to meet other young people of like mind and similar interests.

While she worked for the council, a young man named Mark set his sights on her. He invited her to a movie. I remember this young man knocking at our door. He was nervous, but polite, and he brought Denise back when we asked him to. He asked her out again. This time her Dad wanted more time with him, much to the dismay of Denise.

After our "interrogation" of Mark, we soon recognised that this was a young man with character and that he meant business with Denise. We knew he would not abuse our trust in him and that he had a deep respect for Denise. As parents, we need to be responsible and know whom our children are with. There was no way we would let Denise go out with someone who drove too fast, or who did not treat her with the care and attention we as parents did.

Now, Denise liked Mark too but she was not sure about a long-term relationship and she didn't want to get involved just for dating sake. So many young people go from relationship to relationship and end up fragmenting themselves by giving parts of themselves away to everyone they get involved with. They develop soul ties, which are hard to break. I know young people need to have fun and fellowship, but they can do that in a crowd where there is accountability and safety. That way, should they meet the right person, they enter into that relationship whole and complete.

Mark really courted Denise. He would send flowers, write lovely romantic cards and always made her feel special. He would take her out for meals and treated her like a princess.

When he went on holiday with his friends to Greece he gave Denise a big bag with a present and a card for every day he was away! If you want to score brownie points with girls, treat them real good and court them. Denise fell in love with Mark through his courtship of her.

Their engagement was so romantic. Mark had asked her Dad's and my permission to marry Denise and told us when he was going to propose. Denise thought she was going on an evening out with Mark's parents. We were gob smacked (speechless) when a chauffeur driven Rolls Royce arrived at the door for Denise. Mark was dressed in a white Tux. He took her to a beautiful restaurant where he proposed and had a cake with "Denise, will you marry me?" written on it.

They got engaged in August and got married in June of the following year. Even after the wedding, Mark would think of inventive ways of keeping the romance alive. Mark and Denise married in 1993. To date that's 19 years. They have three children, Joshua, Rebekah and Jessica Joy. Mark still thinks on different ways to surprise and bless them. These things help to keep the romance alive and are a positive demonstration of love in action.

Wives also need to keep the romance in their marriage alive. Don't get into a rut and think that now you have your man, you can let yourself go and become a drudge!

Do the best you can to take care of your appearance. Women's shape change so often with having babies and all the other women things we go through, but no matter how much you weigh, you can still look good.

Lisa Bevere has a great book titled '*You Are Not What You Weigh*'. If you are struggling with your weight or how you see yourself, get this book and apply it to your life. Just reading a book won't change things, but when you start applying it, you will begin to see things changing. Think about what your husband sees when he gets home at night. Remember that he could just have come from his place of work, where the women he works with dress up and take good care of their appearance. I know you may have spent the day running around, gardening, cleaning, looking after the children, but it takes ten minutes to change, brush your hair and put on some lip-gloss. Buy yourself a nice feminine nightdress or pyjamas. Spray on some nice perfume. I go through perfume like water and it's not because I sweat a lot! I just like to smell nice.

You can plan special evenings at home. Sometimes men like to come in from work and just chill. You could make a nice meal or get a Chinese meal sent in, then put on a good movie and snuggle up together.

Go for a night out. Get a baby sitter and have dinner in a nice restaurant. There are lots of things you can plan, without it breaking the bank. It is worth it.

You will get out of your marriage what you put into it. So don't delay in making the changes today.

Every woman wants to marry a prince who is romantic. So often, women don't bring out the best in a man. A man wants to protect, provide and cherish his wife. Woman, let him be that prince.

9

Your Daughter

Titus 2:3–5 (Amplified Bible)

*B*id the older women similarly to be reverent and devout in their deportment as becomes those engaged in sacred service, not slanderers or slaves to drink. They are to give good counsel and be teachers of what is right and noble.

So that they will wisely train the young women to be sane and sober of mind, temperate, disciplined and to love their husbands and their children.

To be self controlled, chaste, (my husband says young women need to remain chaste if they want to be chased!) homemakers, good natured, kind-hearted, adapting and subordinating themselves to their husbands (This does not mean being a door mat, but rather being supportive), that the word of God may not be exposed to reproach, blasphemed or discredited.

Message Bible

Guide older women into lives of reverence so they end up as neither gossips nor drunks, but models of goodness. By looking at them, the younger women will know how to love their husbands and children, be virtuous and pure, keep a good house, and be good wives. We don't want anyone looking down on God's message because of their behaviour.

You need to begin to prepare your daughter for being a wife and a mother early in her life. You are doing her a great disservice if you don't. The teenage stage is when her body begins to change and she is being prepared for childbirth and all that comes with that. Tell her what she can expect to happen in her body, and explain to her the changes she will experience. Tell her she is valuable and should never give her virginity to anyone but her husband. Affirm her as a woman and tell her how beautiful she is. Teach her to be a homemaker, a cook, a mother and whatever else she needs to know, to prepare her for the day she leaves home and cleaves to her husband. She will thank you for it and she will come to you for advice, if, and when she needs it.

I didn't know how to honour my husband when I was first married, but I quickly learned, and have done my best to pass this onto my daughter.

We would have more peace and joy in our homes if we would walk in God's word and be a good wife to our husbands. Our children would see our honour and respect for our husbands and they in turn would honour their fathers and their mothers.

You may not have a daughter in the natural but if you are an older woman, you still have a responsibility to the younger women in your church or in your family. You are to be an example to them, both in word and in deeds. They are to see in you the expression of a woman who loves and follows after Christ and who is loyal to her God, her family and her church.

Don't be a gossip–monger or a complainer. Don't be one who is judgemental and critical. You don't build yourself up by tearing others down. The law of gentleness is to be on our tongue. You will never attract followers by being contentious, which means being argumentative.

Proverbs 22:10 (Amplified Bible)

Drive out the scoffer, and contention will go out, yes strife and abuse will cease.

Proverbs 26:20 (Amplified Bible)

For lack of wood the fire goes out, and where there is no whisperer contention ceases.

Proverbs 25:24 (Amplified Bible)

It is better to dwell in the corner of the housetop than to share a house with a disagreeing, quarrelsome and scolding woman.

Teach your daughter and the young women in your life, to speak positively over others and to avoid gossip, which only leads to hurt, strife, confusion and every evil work.

Build the lives and the marriages of those around you by sharing God's word, giving a listening ear and wise counsel and above all, setting the correct example.

I love the following scripture and encourage you to apply it in all you do.

Proverbs 24:3 & 4 (Amplified Bible)

Through skilful and godly wisdom is a house (a life, a home, a family) built, and by understanding it is established on a sound and good foundation.

And by knowledge shall its chambers (of every area) be filled with all precious and pleasant riches.

10

The Independent Woman

The men were whispering about her behind her back. Since she got the promotion ahead of them, things had changed and they weren't happy with the status quo. She had got to where she was because of sheer hard work and determination and she deserved that promotion. She believed in the equality of the sexes and could out negotiate any man, any day. No man was going to get the better of her again. Once burnt….!

She looked at her watch. It was 6pm. She would be late again picking up her son from after school care. She felt bad about it, but she couldn't get away any earlier so she would make it up to him. She would buy him that new play station game he wanted.

By the time they got home and ate, it was time for him to go to bed. He still wouldn't sleep without a night-light on. He would probably fall asleep watching TV, although, what he watched, she didn't know. As long as it got him off to sleep, that was the main thing. He had stopped asking her to read him stories long ago.

She knew that he missed his Daddy and enjoyed his once a month visits with him, where he was part of the "new family" or blended family. His little half brother was fun to play with and his new step mum had more time for him than she had.

She appeased her conscience with thoughts of how good she was to her son, always providing the best for him. He wore designer clothes, had his own TV, computer, play station, I pod and a room full of the latest toys. Whatever he asked for, she bought him.

The old Beetles song came into her mind. "I don't care too much for money, for money can't buy me love." She started to feel guilty but quickly pushed the thoughts out of her mind. She had hardened her heart against feeling bad about anything she did, even when she knew she was doing wrong. The other women in the office called her 'the bitch' and ice woman. Well, she would make sure she lived up to their expectations of her! To her face they were always polite and courteous, but that was because she was their boss and they knew better than to get on the wrong side of her. She took pride in her position as overseer of the office and was secretly pleased that she intimidated those under her authority. She thrived on her job. It was the most important thing in her life.

It was archaic to expect women to be exclusively wives and mothers. No way was she going to end up like her Mum – divorced, deserted and depressed.

Her mother had brought her up to be independent. "What happened to me will never happen to you" her mother would always say.

Her mother thought that all men were after was sex and someone to keep house for them. It was as if she had been prepared for divorce even before she was married. Her mother had died before she got divorced but she didn't really miss her. She had never really known a mother's love and had no idea of what a loving family relationship should be. She was, for all intents and purposes, motherless and fatherless. The sad thing was, so was her son, but she didn't really see that.

She had divorced her husband four years ago and had custody of their son. If he had been more open to her working after she had the baby, it may have been different. But no, he wanted a wife who would be there when he came home from work and he didn't want his son in a day care centre. What really made her angry was when he berated her for the late nights. She had tried to explain to him that that was part of her remit. She had to entertain clients and take them out for dinner. He had said he had married her because he had wanted a wife, not a company executive.

When she started to earn more than him things started to go from bad to worse. She didn't need him to provide for her. They argued non-stop and she used her body as a tool to get what she wanted. His reward for compliance to her was sex. She had always been able to use that to get her own way. Manipulation and intimidation, he had called it. Didn't every woman do that?

Oh, she was tired. The new guy in sales wasn't like all the others. He seemed to delight in challenging all her decisions. She was doing her best not to get stressed out and insecure about it. Maybe if she slept with him he would soften towards her, but he didn't seem to fancy her.

The headache started. After having faked them for years, it was a shock to actually feel the pain. Maybe her contact lens needed renewing. She would take a sleeping pill. That would help. She had let herself get into the habit of taking them every night, but it was getting harder and harder to get up for work in the morning. She would cope. She was an independent woman and needed neither man nor God.

She didn't believe in the Bible. All those lies about Adam and Eve and a serpent. That was for children, not for successful people like herself. Of course, the woman got the blame, just like everyone blamed her for the divorce and called her a bad mother. What did they know?

She turned off the bedroom light and began to cry. Despite the hard face she wore, she was so lonely and so afraid. She had no friends, because no one trusted her and her co-workers were afraid of her. No one ever hugged her. She needed affection, but even her own son had stopped hugging her. She knew he would be happier with his Dad, but she would not give into that! He was all she had. She would give him everything and he would never leave her. She didn't realise that she was being controlling and manipulative. What were vices to others were to her virtues. She didn't see that her mind was completely messed up. She began to strategise for the next day's board meeting. It was getting more difficult every day to maintain leadership. They needed her there right now and that's what counted. She was indispensable.

She closed her eyes. "Eve didn't have all the pressure I have", she thought… "But I'm an independent woman. I don't need a man, I don't need God, I don't need anyone…

11

Marriage – Part 1
How to Support and Submit

Ill thrives the hapless family that shows
A cock that's silent and a hen that crows
I know not which lives most unnatural lives
Obeying husbands or commanding wives!
(Adam Clarke's Commentary)

Woman was constructed or "built" to be a helper and to complete man. That was her purpose in God's eyes, but because men have abandoned their responsibility as leaders in the home, more and more women are taking on a role they were not created or equipped for. I am not inferring that women are weak or inferior, as women are strong and capable and can take the lead in the home when they have to.

We need to understand that men are under attack from the devil, whose mandate is to destroy marriages and families.

There was to be no competition but completion. Woman is to stand beside her husband and strengthen him with her support.

Ephesians 5:22 (Amplified Bible)

Wives, be subject (be submissive and adapt yourselves) to your own husbands as a service to the Lord.

Verse 25 *For the husband is head of the wife as Christ is the head of the church, Himself the Saviour of His body.*

The Greek meaning of the word submit, is to under gird and support. Just like a bridge needs support, so does a home. To build a home, you need a good foundation and a support structure to hold up the walls and the roof. Your husband cannot fulfil his dreams and goals, without your support. You are to get behind him and help him achieve all that God has for him. You build structure into your marriage and home by getting into agreement as husband and wife, and by being of the same mind whilst speaking the same thing.

Amos 3:3 (Amplified Bible)

Do two walk together except they make an appointment and have agreed?

If there is no agreement with you and your spouse, then it's time to make an appointment to get together and communicate! If you need to discuss situations that may lead to contention and arguments, then I suggest you go somewhere public for a coffee and begin to communicate. Every breakdown in a marriage starts with a communication breakdown. When you are in a public place, you are unlikely to lose it with one another and start shouting and fighting. Just a thought!

Women who believe they are to take on a man's role and be independent of man are selling themselves short. Woman was not built or designed to carry the heavy loads which men can cope with, whether they be weight or stress!

1 Peter 3:7 (First part of the verse)

You husbands must be careful of your wives, being thoughtful of their needs and honouring them as the weaker sex.

This verse is not saying that women are weak, but rather that they are to be treated with consideration.

I have spoken to many young women and asked them what they are looking for in a man. The answers I got back were unanimous. They want to be treated with respect and are looking for men with good manners. They want doors to be opened for them, heavy bags carried for them, to be seated at the table, to be cared for and protected.

Why is this not happening?

One of the reasons is that women want to be treated as being equal to men and they have this independent spirit, which intimidates men and stops them from treating women with courtesy and gentleness.

I love being a woman! I am so glad I wasn't born a man! My husband takes good care of me. He is a good provider and protector, and I need his strength, both physically and emotionally. This does not mean that I am a weak, useless person, who can't do anything for myself, but that together as one, we are a strong team. I have strengths my husband needs and he has strengths that I need. We are to complete one another, as husband and wife. We are both in ministry but we compliment one another. We don't compete with one another. We don't give each other "marks out of ten" for what we do!

Ecclesiastes 4:9-12 (Living Bible)

Two can accomplish more than twice as much as one can, for the results can be much better.

If one falls, the other pulls him up: but if a man falls when he is alone, he's in trouble.

Also, on a cold night, two under the same blanket gain warmth from each other, but how can one be warm alone?

And one standing alone can be attacked and defeated, but two can stand back to back and conquer: Three is even better, for a triple-braided cord is not easily broken.

A husband and wife standing together are a formidable team, which can stand against all odds. The prayer of agreement between husband and wife is one of the most powerful, effective prayers a couple can pray. That is why the enemy would like to cause division (di, meaning two, vision) and disagreement in the home.

When this happens, our prayers are hindered, and then we wonder why we are not getting our prayers answered.

In the work place, there are many professional women who can do the job just as well as, and sometimes even better than a man. There are professions where, because of shortages, women are being encouraged to leave their children in nursery and after school care and get back into the work place.

I understand that there are single parents who need to work to support themselves and their children. There are also single women who choose to remain unmarried and are totally content in their career and with their singleness. Every one has to make their choice concerning whether to work or not when they have young children and it would be wrong to condemn them for that. I do believe however, that some women work because they are not content at home and cannot settle into the role of wife and mother. When I have asked them why they work when there is no necessity to do so, the reply has been that staying at home is boring, or they can't cope with their children and so opt for full time work.

My husband and I immigrated to South Africa from Scotland in 1975. Our two boys were aged six and four and our daughter was one and a half years old. At that time in Scotland, it was very unusual for mothers to go out to work unless they were involved in a profession. This was the mindset I had, but because of necessity, I found myself having to go back to work when we arrived in South Africa. We went through a financially difficult period. We were not Christians then and had no concept of believing God for our provision. We did do some praying though!

Before I was married, I worked in a drawing office as a tracer / draftswoman and was able to get a position in a drawing office which paid quite well. Our oldest son was at school till 2pm but I had to put our other two children into a nursery. Our son would come home from school and a neighbour would look after him till I got home.

We had no family to help us but fortunately, we had good neighbours. It was a very difficult time and the children did suffer because I had to work. They did not like it when I was not there for them when they got home from school. They also missed the close family relationships they had when we lived in Scotland. My having to work made the adjustments they had to make that much more difficult. I did eventually get a part time job and was home for them coming in from school.

Our children have since shared some of the thoughts and feelings they experienced through that time, some of which were not easy for me to hear. They did understand why I had to work and they don't hold anything against us as parents, for which I am thankful. I do have regrets and if I had to do it over again, I would do it differently.

We all have to make hard choices at times, but I know that God will help us if we go to Him in prayer.

Our daughter has three children. She had a great job, which she enjoyed, but she chose not to go back to work when her oldest son was born. It meant she had to do without some things and she had to "tighten her belt" when it came to finances, but she has no regrets. She and her husband Mark oversee our nursery to youth ministry in the church and they are a support to my husband and me. Their children are at school full day, so she can now help Mark in the church office. She enjoys being a wife and a mother, yet she is still able to be involved in ministry, which she also enjoys. There is a correct timing to everything. Don't be too anxious to get back into the work place, unless you know without a doubt that it is God's will for you.

If your husband is not in agreement with you working, then you need to listen to him and be content until there is agreement. Ask God to lead you and guide you in this and be led by peace. Remember that physically, there is only so much you can do. Many young women go around feeling exhausted and stressed because of trying to run a home and keep down a full time position at work. Don't burn yourself out. Make the choice to put your family before your job. You are no good to anyone wore out and tired. Stress will age you and you will lose the joy of life and love. If you lose your joy, you lose your goods!

My husband says everyone should do what he or she loves and love what they do. I love being a wife and a mother. I love being a minister alongside my husband. I love being a grandmother. I do what I love and I love what I do.

But, my family is more important to me than ministry. My husband and children come first before church. And of course my relationship with God, Jesus and the Holy Spirit are first place in my life.

Some women have a hard time putting their family before their ministry. Their lives revolve round what they do in church and for the church, and sadly their families are neglected. Many times this becomes a stumbling block to husbands and children. This oughtn't to be so. God's will for you, as a wife, is to minister first to your husband. Don't put your children before him in order of priority. You are only a steward of your children. One day they will leave and then they will cleave!

I know so many women who try to relive their lives through their children. When the children grow up and leave home, the wife finds herself alone with this stranger called her husband. No wonder there are so many divorces when the children leave home. Our children are all married with children of their own and my husband and I are enjoying our lives together. We still help them when they ask us and they know we are always there for them, but we now have the freedom to do what we want to do as a couple. We live an exciting life, full of new and wonderful adventures in faith. We get to minister together and share our wisdom and experience with others. We see God move in mighty ways in our family, church and nation.

We pray that our children will make the right choices in life based on Godly wisdom. But we are not responsible for them any longer. They now stand accountable to God for themselves and their children.

Women, get out of the guilt and condemnation zone and into the freedom zone! You are free to be the wife and mother God created you to be. You are free to be the woman of influence in your workplace that God created you to be. But don't throw away your femininity and your position as helpmeet and completer because of media marketing and peer pressure. In God's eyes, men and women are equal so we don't have to prove anything. We were purpose built for man and we are man's completion.

You are a female by birth and a woman by choice.

12

The Betrayed Woman

The sun warmed her face as she stepped out from the shade of the tree. The barbecue she was hosting was a great success and all her guests were lying around on the lawn talking and laughing. It was a lovely day and the atmosphere was relaxing.

She had been complimented on the food, the bright and colourful table settings and the great music playing in the background. She had hired a DJ to play sixties music and it was going down well with every age group there. The younger couples seemed to enter into the swing of the music and some of them were trying to get the hang of the twist.

'Come on let's twist again" was booming out over the airwaves. She wondered if Chubby Checker was still around. She was fifty–six years old but didn't look a day over forty–two. She paid the price to keep her looks and her figure with her weekly workouts at the gym and a low fat diet. She had a sweet tooth but managed to overcome her desire for chocolate and sweets by banning them from her home. Her family and friends knew not to give her sweets and gave her flowers instead. She loved flowers and there was always an abundance of them around the house.

As she mingled with her guests, she was also keeping an eye out for her husband. He would probably be talking business or golf with his friends and associates. Socialising was part of his remit. His position as sales manager with the company he worked for required him not only to entertain clients and prospective clients but also to have his sales team around. He believed in building good relationships with his team and this had paid off. They exceeded their sales target every month and were rewarded with days like today or dinners and theatre.

She caught his eye and he smiled at her. He mouthed the words, "Wonderful job" and winked at her. She knew he appreciated the hard work and effort she put into these events. She waved at him and moved on. There was a chair at the far side of the garden, which overlooked the valley below her house. It was a great view and so peaceful to look upon. She needed a few minutes on her own. Tiredness came on her suddenly. It wasn't easy being the perfect wife, hostess and mother.

She went into the house and lay down on her bed. She wasn't going to let her thoughts go further but as always, she let her mind carry her back to the day her whole world was shaken.

She hadn't been well that day and had just returned home from the doctors when she realised she had locked herself out of the house. She couldn't believe how stupid she was for not putting her key in her bag. Her husband was forever telling her to put the door key on the same key ring as her car keys, but she hadn't got round to it.

She thought about how that "I told you so" smug look would come on him when she told him and that made her laugh. She had a great marriage and a great husband who loved and cared for her so much. Some of her friends had gone through divorce and some were unhappy in their marriage. She thanked God for her husband and for her marriage. She was blessed and she knew it.

She wasn't feeling too good and wanted to get to bed and rest. The doctor had told her she had some sort of virus and the best cure was plenty of fluids and lots of rest.

This wasn't her day!

Her mobile phone needed topped up, so she couldn't call her husband and arrange to get his key. She decided she would drive round to his office and surprise him. It was only ten minutes away. She walked past the front desk and made her way to the lift. The receptionist normally called through to her husband and let him know she was coming but she wanted to surprise him. She got out of the lift at the top floor executive level. Up there with the high flyers!

Her husband's secretary wasn't at her desk, so she walked into his office without the usual protocol.

She wished she hadn't.

Her husband and his secretary were locked in a passionate embrace and didn't even hear her come in. Time froze and she froze. She couldn't get her mouth to utter a sound. She was in shock.

They must have become aware that she was there because they quickly pulled apart. The secretary ran out of the office and down the stairs out of the building. "I came for the door key. I locked myself out and I wasn't feeling well. The doctor says it's a virus." She was sobbing now and talking incoherently. Why was she apologising for being there? She wasn't the one who was in the wrong. The phrase "being in the wrong place at the wrong time" came to her mind. But she believed that it was fate that had brought her there at that specific time. She felt utterly betrayed and rejected. The word devastated would not have been too strong an adjective to describe the emotions that she was experiencing. Her husband came over to her and put his hands on her shoulders as he ushered her to his chair. "I'm so sorry" He said over and over.

He took her home and put her to bed. She couldn't stop crying. She had a fever and every part of her body ached but her heart was broken and she thought it would never heal again.

He slept in the guest room that night and for some time after. She couldn't bear him near her, let alone touching her. She would try to put it out of her mind, but she kept getting flashbacks and no matter how hard she tried, she could not find it in her heart to forgive her husband.

She confronted him and demanded to know the extent of the relationship. He told her it had ended. It was his first and only affair and it had been brief. He assured her that she was the only person he had ever loved and that it would never happen again, but she had lost her trust in him and didn't know if she could ever trust him again.

It would never happen again, he kept affirming over and over. He loved only her and had been a fool to mess around. He had a new secretary, an older woman who would be no distraction. He accepted the full blame and asked for her forgiveness.

But how could she believe him? How could she ever trust him again? How could she make love to him again? How could she love him? She couldn't. Not in her own strength.

They say time heals, but she still had issues to deal with and work through. She supposed they could go for marriage counselling, but she wouldn't broach the subject with him, and he had never mentioned it. They had started communicating again, at first haltingly, testing the waters.

They put a face on for the sake of their family and friends but it wasn't easy to maintain an atmosphere of peace in the home.

The anger and hurt would rise up in her and all she wanted to do was vent that anger on him and punish him, so he would suffer the way she was suffering. She would think up ways to get at him, but she never voiced these things or acted on them. She knew if she did, she would never stop and it would be the end of their marriage. And deep down she didn't want that to happen.

She knew she would have to put it all behind her and move on. She had tried so hard but it wasn't happening. Her marriage was all pretence. She had become embittered and had hardened her heart towards her husband. All she wanted was for things to be the way they were before his affair. It wasn't fair. She didn't deserve this.

Her mind was in turmoil again. God, how she needed peace. Other women coped with their husband's affairs and got on with their lives. Why couldn't she? "God help me" she cried. "Help me to love and trust my husband again. Give me the desire for him again." Deep down on the inside, she knew what she had to do. She had to forgive him. But it was too hard. No, she would never forgive him. It was something she could never do – no, not could, but would never do!

She turned her head towards the wall next to her bed. Everyone must have left and she had fallen asleep. Her husband had gone to bed. She could hear his breathing slow and steady, coming from the guest bedroom but even though her body cried out with need for him, she resisted the desire for him.

She knew she was choosing not to bring restoration to her marriage. She knew she was probably driving her husband to seek after someone else, more loving, more giving. Forgiveness? He didn't deserve it.

Did he?

13

Marriage _ Part 2
Building a Marriage

God's plan was that for every man there would be one woman. Promiscuity causes confusion. When man and woman marry, they enter into a covenant, which is an agreement or contract. They leave their father and mother and cleave (stick together) to one another. Commitment is the glue of marriage.

Marriage was ordained by God to be enjoyed. Pleasure first, then children. Marriage comes in kit form and is a joint building project, which requires husband and wife working at the relationship together. Good marriages happen on purpose.

One out of every two marriages ends in divorce and many more suffer from neglect, betrayal and lies. These statistics are an indication of just how far we have strayed from healthy and stable family units and core values. There are so many things that come against marriages, negative forces from within the relationship and from outside the home. Sometimes this can be from the in-laws. I have worked through many challenges in my marriage and have had to put a lot of work into keeping it stable and successful. If you think you can neglect your relationship with your spouse and still have a good marriage, you are mistaken. I had a lot of decisions to make, such as; choosing to love my husband when I didn't feel like it, forgiving him when I felt like murder, humbling myself when I knew I was right!! We all have experience of that one!

I had to learn to be selfless and not selfish. Before you enter into marriage you have to understand that it is no longer going to be all about you. When you say "I do" it brings a new dimension into your life. You can no longer consider what you want to do but what would both of you want to do. Compatibility goes a long way to making marriage easier. For instance, if your husband is into the great outdoors and you can't stand that, then there are going to be challenges and a lot of give and take. (And that doesn't mean he does all the giving and you do all the taking!)

Unity in the Marriage

Right from the beginning of creation, God's mind was set on unity. In fact, the triune Godhead was fully unified in creation. After God created man, He says this in *Genesis 2:18* "*It is not good that man should be alone...*" In that one statement we see God's heart for unity. He goes on to make Eve from Adam's side. In doing so, God creates a family dynamic. He creates unity as one of the highest values of all creation. Once Eve arrived everything was wonderful. She was happy,

Adam was happy, God was pleased, but then, you can read in chapter 3 of Genesis, Satan comes to Eve with a temptation. She falls for it and the decision to sin causes separation from God. This is what Satan desired most, to separate man from God and bring division between husband and wife. Division and separation are his oldest tricks and he has not changed. Disunity brings ineffectiveness and unfruitfulness. Division brings with it defeat and divorce.

1 Corinthians 1:10

Now I plead with you, brethren, by the name of the Lord Jesus Christ, that you speak the same thing, and that there be no divisions among you, but that you be perfectly joined together in the same mind and in the same judgement.

Unity brings victory and that is God's plan for your marriage.

Matthew 18:19–20

Again I say to you that if two of you agree on earth concerning anything that they ask, it will be done for them by My Father in Heaven. For where two or three are gathered together in My name, I am there in the midst of them.

Wherever there is strife and division, Satan is present. Wherever unity exists, God is right there in the middle of that unity and in that, He commands a blessing. If you want God at the centre of your home, then you better start working towards unity with your spouse.

The power of unity is the power to succeed at whatever you set your mind, heart or hands to do. A house divided cannot stand, but a house united can accomplish anything.

As a minister, my husband won't marry any couple unless they agree to pre-marital counselling. He gives them a questionnaire they have to fill in separately and truthfully. They are not allowed to discuss this with one another. By reading through their answers, he can see clearly the areas that need to be addressed. Many times couples think they have agreement on certain points, but in reality a lot of it is presumption. One of the questions asked is "Have you agreement on having children?" On one occasion the woman had answered that question by saying, yes they had agreement, and had decided they would not have children. The man answered, yes they had agreement, and they wanted children. When this was flagged up to them, the woman said that they had discussed it and she was assured that there would be no children, but the man's understanding was that they had discussed it and would have children after a time.

In this instance the couple decided not to go ahead with the wedding. Had they done so, they would have faced certain conflict which would have led to divorce. We did hear later that both of them had met other partners and were now happily married. We have testimonies from many of the couples in our church as to how helpful the pre-marital counselling was to them. Issues which could lead to a breakdown in the marriage were highlighted and dealt with at the counselling sessions and a good foundation was laid on which to build upon. I strongly advise all couples who are getting married to go to their minister and get pre-marital counselling. You will benefit greatly from it and it will help you to set your short and long term goals and open up lines of communication that you may not have entered into. Don't be afraid that it may hinder the wedding plans. The opposite is true – it will be exciting and enjoyable.

When I got married, there was nothing like pre-marital counselling available, so I had no help or advice as to how to be a good wife or what to expect from my husband. I had many unrealistic expectations of what marriage was about and not living a God centred life at the time, I experienced many difficult times throughout those first years of my marriage.

Bernie and I met in 1964 and we married in 1967. We were both eighteen years old when we got married, were not Christians and had no idea of what covenant was about. We see it as a miracle of God that we stayed together through those tumultuous first years. We both came from stable backgrounds where our parents were together. Bernie was born second in line of ten and I was the eldest of five. Without God we were heading for disaster, but we didn't know that then!

By the time I was twenty-one, we had two sons and three years later our daughter was born. In 1975 we emigrated from Scotland to South Africa and it was there in 1979 that we became Christians.

Looking back on that time before 1979, I have so many regrets. I was young and naive and definitely not the ideal wife or mother, but thank God for His love and acceptance, I can go on without guilt or condemnation. This is so important – not only in having a healthy marriage but also in living a healthy lifestyle. We cannot afford to always live with the memory of past mistakes and in regret. We need to remember that every day is new and that God's mercies are new every morning. I thank God for that, as I use more than my fair share of mercies every day! By the time tomorrow comes I need new mercies!

For two people to become one flesh, both have to make changes. Of course, I thought he was the one who was always wrong and that I was perfect. I would work out ways to "change" him into the man I thought he should be! Thank God I got smart and changed my way of thinking. Only God can change the heart of a person through the agent of the Holy Spirit.

I knew things would have to change if our marriage was to survive. I learned not to wait on my husband, with an "I will if you will" attitude! I made the decision that I was going to change regardless of what he did. I humbled myself and chose to let my pride go and find that when I do that, God lifts me up and gives me the grace I need to change.

Previously, I was selfish and wanted things to go my way, so I would use emotional manipulation to get my own way. I had regular "'pity parties'" and frequent "temper tantrums". On my 19th birthday, Bernie bought me a lovely gold plated pendant, as he couldn't afford the real thing then! He had been working that day and had got home late. I was so upset at him being late that I threw the pendant at the wall. He was so mad he went out with his friends and I was left at home feeling so sorry for myself. I cried the whole night. When he got home we made up and the next day we got on with our life. However, I had hurt him. There were times when he would hurt me by saying things he didn't really mean. Over the years these hurts can become walls between husbands and wives that need to be torn down. Words have the power to wound and can leave scars that can take a lifetime to heal, so make the decision to always be gracious in your speech and speak words that are life giving.

Our first house was a cottage with dampness running down the walls. We couldn't light a fire because the chimney smoked. David was just a baby and I can remember him sitting in his pram in his wee fur coat. We didn't have any money and we were thankful for our parents helping us out from time to time. I could clean house but I wasn't much of a cook. We survived on scrambled egg or fish fingers and chips. The only time we ate anything nourishing was when we visited our parents as eating out for us wasn't an option, unless it was a fish supper!

There are so many stories I could share of those early days. One time a greyhound dog followed Bernie home from work. I didn't want the hound hanging around so I made him go out and chase it away. After our dinner of egg and chips, Bernie started reading our local paper. In the ad section there was a reward notice which read: Reward of £10 (This was more than a week's wages then) for greyhound, call such and such telephone number. Bernie took great pleasure in reading it out loud to me of course, and I sent him out with instructions to find the animal or else! He never did find that dog!

We had fun too, and by accident, not design, we did manage to stay together and bring up our children. We recognise now that God had His hand upon our family and He kept us for His purpose.

Bernie and the children became Christians one year after me in 1980, and we joined a church. Our decision for Christ is the best thing we have ever done. Prior to that, we were heading for divorce. At that time, Bernie was consumed with his job and was climbing the promotion ladder at work, becoming the top sales man and the director's blue-eyed boy! A big part of his remit was entertaining customers. This involved food and drink and partying. He worked late and sometimes I was already in bed when he got home so there was a lot of pressure on our relationship. I was working in a large drawing office and getting lots of attention from the guys who worked beside me.

Women, beware of getting involved with the men you work beside. I have seen so many marriages end up in divorce because the wife had an affair with someone she worked with. If you get to the place where you are dressing up for the men in your work and not your husband, you are in the danger zone.

Believe me, it is not worth it. The grass is not greener on the other side. You may think your husband is ugly and bad tempered etc, etc, etc, but, I can assure you, there is another woman out there who would love to be in your shoes! Appreciate your husband and honour him and your marriage vows by not flirting around with other men. It may be a game to you but it's not to the men! You can't play with fire and not be burned.

Date–rape drugs are on the increase and many women have no recollection of what happened to them while they were out partying with the crowd at work. With sexually transmitted diseases on the increase, the repercussions of sexual promiscuity are so real and so dangerous. Many women cannot conceive because of STD's. That is why fertility treatment is on the increase. You may only have had one sexual partner in your life, but how many has the guy had? Only one? How many partners did that one have? Get smart. It really is not worth it, spiritually, emotionally and physically.

I thank God for His protection over me all those years ago, for I could have so easily got into an affair. There but for the grace of God go I.

To be honest, we actually made the decision to stay together before we became Christians. Deep down in our hearts there was a love and commitment for one another and we had gone through so many hard times already, that we knew we would be making a huge mistake if we divorced. It was the week after a particularly big argument that we went to church for the first time and the rest is history!

Strife and separation could still come between us if we let it, but we have learned to talk things over and be open and honest with one another without getting into an argument. My husband calls arguing intense fellowship. So we never argue but can get intense sometimes!

Communication is Vital to Having a Strong Marriage

Our communication has improved so much over the years. Firstly, we now take the time to communicate. This involves listening as well as talking. I am still brushing up on my listening skills. As a minister working alongside my husband, I am so used to giving out information and counsel to others and I had to learn when to keep quiet and let him speak. You have to communicate clearly and effectively and also let your husband express himself. Communication takes time and can't be rushed. Not only does it take time but it also has to be the right time! Wanting to discuss issues while he is watching his favourite sport on TV is not a good time! Pick the time and the place.

When I need to talk to my husband, I ask him out on a date and go somewhere quiet where there are no distractions. It makes such a difference and both of us are far more relaxed and much less defensive. If you have young children then ask a friend or family member to baby sit so you can both go out somewhere to talk. Children demand attention and to communicate effectively, your attention needs to be solely on each other.

Have a regular time when you get together and discuss your day and what you are working on. Talk about the people you met and whom you visited that day. Life can get hectic and days, sometimes even weeks can go by without husband and wife really communicating. It's always best to go out somewhere for coffee if you have issues to discuss. You are less likely to have a stand up fight in a public place! Make the time and be gentle with one another, in attitude, actions and in speech.

Proverbs 15:4 (Amplified Bible)

A gentle tongue with its healing power is a tree of life, but wilful contrariness in it breaks down the spirit.

Most of the arguments we have had are because of bad communication. He assumes I know about things and thinks he has told me about appointments and the like. Meanwhile, I don't have a clue. Either he forgot to tell me, or I wasn't listening properly to him, or I forgot!

There are times we have gone out on our own to have a nice evening together, which doesn't happen very often. You would think we should have everything organised and have a wonderful romantic evening planned. Not so! We get in the car and he says to me "what would you like to do sweetheart? I reply "Whatever you would like to do darling" This goes back and forth and pretty soon the sweetheart and darling are dropped from the conversation! We end up going somewhere that neither of us likes, and when eventually we admit this, I will say "I thought you would want to do this". He would say "No, I thought you would like it here". We find ourselves having a miserable time trying to please one another. Ever been there, done that, bought the shirt? Of course, that doesn't happen as frequently now!

Always be open and honest with each other. Tell each other what you like and what you don't like. Get into agreement about where you go and what you want to do. Now there are times when we need to be unselfish and do some stuff together that is maybe out of your comfort zone. My husband is a keen golfer and really enjoys the game. I encourage him to go out and golf, as it is great relaxation for him. There are times when he asks me to walk round the course with him. Now I may not feel like it, but I know it means a lot to him, so I go. I am actually thinking about taking the game up so we can play golf together. You have been warned in advance. Beware of stray golf balls flying your way!!

My husband also does things with me. Like shopping, etc, etc, etc. He is long suffering and doesn't moan but has a lot of empathy with the guys he sees sitting outside the changing rooms, who grunt something when their wife asks them if they look good in the outfit they are trying on! "Does it suit me sweetheart?" "Grunt". "Does it make me look fat?" "Grunt, grunt." "It only costs a few hundred pounds." "What?"(Imagine steam coming out of his ears). That will get their attention!

Support and Encourage One Another

Men need to be encouraged and built up by their wives, not brow beaten or broken down. They don't need to be constantly reminded of their mistakes and failures but rather, that God is with them, in them and that all things are possible with God. Let your husband know that you are for him and not against him. If you will do this you will see him rise above difficult situations. Choose to be a partner who exudes faith and hope in your husband. Be his champion and support him. Stay loyal always and watch and see what great things God will do in and for your family.

Bernie and I have learned to really love each other but we needed to learn how to love ourselves first. You can't love others if you can't love yourself. If you are looking for a man so that you can feel complete, then you will face disappointment. Before we enter a marriage, a life long relationship, we have to be complete in ourselves. This is only possible by having the Spirit of God living in us. Christianity is dying to self and living for Christ. (God's love between two people causes them to adapt and be at peace.) A Christ–centred marriage will always be a successful marriage. We should be subject to one another out of reverence for Christ. Two becoming one is a daily process. It won't happen overnight.

Built To last

As women we must build our marriages to last. We need to stop treating each other the way we feel like and start preferring one another in love, the way God commands us to. That simply means putting our spouse first.

Proverbs 31 gives us an example of a woman revered by the way in which she lived out her life as a wife and mother. It gives us an example of how a wise woman builds her house. You won't find this woman in any one person, but she represents the different godly traits we should be exercising in our lives.

* Keep your marriage and your home Christ centred.
* Be led by the Holy Spirit daily.
* Remember that marriage in itself won't bring you happiness.
* You carry happiness into your marriage.
* Learn to laugh and have a sense of humour. It will carry you both through some tense situations.

I love this scripture from the Living Bible.

Psalm 101:2

I will try to walk a blameless path. But oh, how I need your help, especially in my own home, where I long to act as I should.

We all want to do the right thing. How many times have you heard someone say "But God knows my heart'? We can't use that as an excuse not to discipline ourselves and to be disobedient to the leading of the Holy Spirit in our lives. Those who are led by the Spirit will not fulfil the leanings of the flesh.

To walk a blameless path, we need God's help.

Today could be a turning point in your life as a married woman. Decide now to let God work in and through you and give control of your life and your marriage to Him. Don't have an independent spirit.

14

Dealing with Divorce

There is hardly a family in the United Kingdom today that has not been touched by divorce. In our church we have many families who have been through divorce and as a result, have stepchildren, some of whom live with them. Having counselled many couples and helped them through the difficult stages of a failed marriage, I am thankful for God's grace and His wisdom, which enables my husband and I to do this.

Without that, we would only be able to deal with things in the natural, and divorce has to do with spirit, soul and body.

Most people ask me the same questions regarding divorce and in the light of that, this will be a chapter which deals with these most asked questions. Your particular situation may be different, but generally, I have found that people face the same challenges and heartache when dealing with divorce.

Is Divorce A Sin?

God's will is to set at liberty those who are bruised, poor, broken-hearted and bound. I was always told that divorce was a sin and that if you were divorced you couldn't remarry. Some marriages break down and don't work out and if yours didn't, then don't condemn yourself, sadly, it happens to a lot of folks. We encourage couples to do all they can to work at their marriage and try to save it, but because of people's free will choices, that does not always work. My husband performs marriage ceremonies for couples that have been divorced, his only condition being, they partake of pre-marital counselling. The reason for this is to help them deal with unresolved issues. The last thing anyone wants is to bring baggage into a new relationship.

Marriage is a Spiritual Union

Two people become one flesh in the sight of God.

Matthew 19:6

What God has joined together, let not man put asunder.

It is the spirit of man and woman that God joins together, not the flesh. The act of making love is an expression of marriage. Until people understand that marriage is a uniting of spirit and not of flesh, separation and divorce will continue, in the church and out of it. In the eyes of God, marriage is forever. Divorce is not just the dissolving of a partnership, but the separation of two spirits and that is a decision made in the heart by either one or both partners in marriage.

I believe one of the reasons for divorce today is ignorance of the fact that marriage is spiritual first and foremost. As a married Christian woman, I have to commit to my marriage and walk in the fruit of the Spirit towards my husband. I can do no less, no matter what I feel like!

Sin is defined as a selfish decision that displeases God. We know what pleases God and what doesn't and we have to do our best to please Him.

Hebrews 11:6 says that *"faith pleases God."*

We need to apply faith in our marriage and faith in our spouse and trust God for the best outcome. This is not always easy and we don't always have the final say in the outcome, but we do need to know that we have done all we could to save our marriage. So then, if you have done all you could, but the marriage still failed, trust God with your future, and move on. You cannot remain under the bondage of guilt and shame and expect to live a full life. If however, the decision to divorce was a selfish one and you knew that you should not have done it, you need to ask God to forgive you, receive His forgiveness, and move on. Put the past behind you and make the decision to be led by God in your relationships and in your life.

Sin is conceived in the heart and then acted upon. There are many couples that are still legally married but divorced in their spirit. They live in the same house but have no relationship with one another. In God's eyes, they have separated. They may deceive others, but they can't deceive themselves and God. A good healthy marriage requires both partners giving of themselves and submitting to God's will in their relationship.

What about Adultery?

Jesus understood the situation of adultery completely.

Mathew 5:27–32

You have heard that it was said to those of old, you shall not commit adultery.

But I say to you that whoever looks at a woman to lust for her has already committed adultery with her in his heart.

And if your right eye causes you to sin, pluck it out and cast it from you; for it is more profitable for you that one of your members perish, than for your whole body to be cast into hell.

And if your right hand causes you to sin, cut it off and cast it from you; for it is more profitable for you that one of your members perish, than for your whole body to be cast into hell.

Furthermore, it has been said, whoever divorces his wife for any reason except sexual immorality causes her to commit adultery; and whoever marries a woman who is divorced commits adultery.

Matthew 19:1–9

Now it came to pass, when Jesus finished these sayings, that He departed from Galilee and came into the region of Judea beyond the Jordan.

And great multitudes followed Him, and He healed them there.

The Pharisees also came to him, testing Him, and saying to him, "Is it lawful for a man to divorce his wife for just any reason?"

And He answered and said to them, "Have you not read that He who made them at the beginning, made them male and female?"

And said, For this reason a man shall leave his father and mother and be joined to his wife, and the two shall become one flesh.

So then, they are no longer two but one flesh. Therefore, what God has joined together, let no man separate.

They said to him, "Why then did Moses command to give a certificate of divorce, and to put her away?"

He said to them, Moses, because of the hardness of your hearts, permitted you to divorce your wives, but from the beginning it was not so.

And I say to you, whoever divorces his wife, except for sexual immorality, and marries another, commits adultery; and whoever marries her who is divorced commits adultery.

John 8 verses 1 to 11 deals with the woman taken in the act of adultery. Jesus should have stoned the woman, but He didn't, which shows us God's view of the whole subject.

Adultery is defined as: Violation of the marriage bed, sexual intercourse between a married man and woman, not his wife, or visa versa. Adultery is a common legal ground for divorce. Adultery is a sin and everyone knows that. But we see that Jesus forgave that woman and told her to go and sin no more. If you have committed adultery, repent, ask God to forgive you, and go and sin no more. Jesus came to redeem us from all our sin regardless of what that may be. We have to receive His forgiveness in an attitude of humility and true repentance. If you are divorced as a result of adultery, there is absolution, and you can move forward knowing that there is no condemnation to those who walk after the Spirit and not the flesh. With this in mind, you can remarry if you so wish if you know you have met the right person. Be up front with them and let them know you have put things right with God. Make sure you have someone you can be accountable to.

We have a Men's Ministry called 'Repairers of the Breach', which my husband founded in 2002. He is a spiritual father to many pastors, leaders and men. He has men go through a process of mentoring and accountability, which has been very fruitful. We have seen men rise up and take their place as husbands, fathers and leaders. Much of the success is due to the mutual accountability the men have with each other.

It is the same with the ladies mentoring process I have in the church. Where there is accountability, sin and temptation can have no power over you. The power of sin is in its hiddeness. When the light of God's word shines on sin, it loses its power. When you open yourself up to someone and expose the sin that you are struggling with, you put yourself on the path to victory.

If you have been in an adulterous relationship, after you have received forgiveness, you need to find someone you can go to if the temptation should ever arise. Don't deceive yourself by thinking you are above this. We know the battle is in the mind, and when the wrong thoughts come, we have to immediately deal with them through the word of God. Of course, you need to choose wisely who that person will be, but ask the Holy Spirit to give you the connection and He will.

What about the Past?

Make sure you have forgiven your ex-spouse so that you can move on with your life. Unforgiveness will cause you to become a bitter person and no one will want to befriend you. God has given you the capacity to release forgiveness. Jesus said that if we don't forgive others, then God cannot forgive us. It's not worth risking our relationship with God for anything.

The bible makes it clear that offences shall surely come, but you can choose not to pick up the offence.

Mark 11:25–26

And when you stand praying, if you have anything against anyone, forgive him, that your Father in heaven may also forgive you, your trespasses. But if you do not forgive, neither will your father in heaven forgive your trespasses.

Ephesians 4:24, 31, 32

Put on the NEW MAN. Let all bitterness, and wrath, and anger, and clamour, and evil speaking, be put away from you, with all malice.

And be kind to one another, tenderhearted, forgiving one another, even as God for Christ's sake has forgiven you.

If you harbour bitterness in your heart towards an ex-spouse, with time, you will lump all men into the same category, and your hurt will degenerate into bitterness.

Why is it difficult for people to forgive?

Emotional pain can be so hard and because of the trauma many find it hard to forgive. They hurt not only themselves, but also their families and the children of the failed marriage. These emotional scars go from generation to generation and the only way to break the iniquity is through releasing forgiveness and repenting of the bitterness. God can heal and restore.

I have experienced the power of restoration in my own family. Our son was married for ten years and had two children. Sadly his marriage failed and he got divorced. It was a very difficult time for all of us as a family. My husband and I did all we could to be supportive and bring stability and peace into the lives of our grandchildren. We did not pick up his, or his ex wife's offence and we chose to walk in forgiveness. God's grace was upon us and today we are thankful for that.

Our son has since married a lovely Christian woman, who loves him very much and has accepted the children. God has restored to him a marriage and family and we are thankful that our grandchildren are still serving God and stable and secure. To receive this restoration our son had to forgive himself and all other people involved. If he had not done this he would still be living with the guilt and shame of divorce and the anger and bitterness that comes with this. There is life after divorce, so don't give up hope. Choose to forgive and be liberated.

When Adultery Continues

If your spouse has committed adultery and is not repentant, you can divorce him and remarry if you so choose.

Matthew 19:4–9 (New King James Version)

And He answered and said to them, Have you not read that he who made them at the beginning, made them male and female.

And said, For this reason a man shall leave his father and mother and be joined to his wife, and the two shall become one flesh.

So then, they are no longer two but one flesh. Therefore what God has joined together let no man separate.

They said to Him, Why then did Moses command to give a certificate of divorce, and to put her away.

He said to them, Moses, because of the hardness of your hearts, permitted you to divorce your wives, but from the beginning it was not so.

And I say to you, whoever divorces his wife, except for sexual immorality, and marries another, commits adultery: and whoever marries her who is divorced commits adultery.

Adultery is a scriptural reason for divorce and the person sinned against is under no obligation to continue with the marriage. I would like to reiterate that if the one in adultery repents and wants to work at the marriage then this should be prayed over before taking the step to divorce.

What Happens if My Unbelieving Husband Leaves Me?

1 Corinthians 7:12–17 (Message Bible)

For the rest of you who are in mixed marriages, Christian married to a non-Christian; we have no explicit command from the Master. So this is what you must do. If you are a man with a wife who is not a believer but who still wants to live with you, hold on to her. If you are a woman with a husband who is not a believer but he wants to live with you, hold on to him. The unbelieving husband shares to an extent in the holiness of his wife, and the unbelieving wife is likewise touched by the holiness of her husband. Otherwise your children would be left out, as it is, they also are included in the spiritual purposes of God.

On the other hand, if the unbelieving spouse walks out, you've got to let him or her go. You don't have to hold on desperately. God has called us to make the best of it, as peacefully as we can. You never know, wife: The way you handle this might bring your husband not only back to you but to God.

You never know husband: The way you handle this might bring your wife not only back to you but to God.

And don't be wishing you were someplace else or with someone else. Where you are right now is God's place for you. Love and obey and love and believe right there. God, not your marital status, defines your life. Don't think I'm being harder on you than on the others. I give this same counsel in all the churches.

Verse 13 in the New King James translation says:

And a woman who has a husband, who does not believe, if he is willing to live with her, let her not divorce him.

If an unbelieving wife is running around with other men then she is not pleased to live with her husband. If an unbelieving husband is beating and abusing his wife, then he's not pleased to live with her. When a woman is being physically abused we do not recommend she stays with her husband, whether he is saved or not!

The Christian wife is not under bondage to the marriage vows. She can marry again, in the Lord. I feel sorry for women who choose to stay in abusive situations. They think that by submitting to the abuse they can get their husbands saved. If you could do that then Paul would have said so in the above scriptures. You might get your husband saved, but you might not. It is still his choice and if God can't make him repent and get saved, then what makes you think you can? Many women suffer through things and put their children through things because they think they must stay with their husbands. If the unbelieving husband is happy to stay with his Christian wife, then she should stay and be the best wife she can to him.

1 Peter 3:1 (New King James Version)

Likewise you wives, be submissive to your own husbands, that even if some do not obey the word, they, without a word, may be won by the conduct of their wives.

Even if your husband is unsaved, he is still the head of the house. Unless he is asking you to wilfully sin, you are to love and honour him. Many men get turned off when their wives try to "Lord" it over them. Don't be so spiritual that your husband can't touch you. Love and enjoy your marriage and you will see that man come to Christ. I have seen this happen time and time again, when the wife esteems her husband and gives him his place. If you are a Christian, you should be more loving as a wife because you have the God kind of love in your spirit.

I Chose the Wrong Husband!

You can't unscramble eggs! Many women have come to me wanting a divorce based on incompatibility. They say they have nothing in common with their husbands and they should never have got married.

I got married in 1967 when I had just turned eighteen. I was naive and hadn't a clue what I was committing to when I said yes to my young, handsome eighteen year old husband! After the "in love" stage wore off, I thought I had totally blown it! I began to doubt if I had made the right choice. We were both unsaved at the time and had no spiritual guidance or counselling prior to our marriage. However, as young as I was, I had literally made my bed and I literally had to lie on it! Both sets of parents were of that mindset and we knew they wouldn't take us back! We had to get on with it and do the best we could. I truly believe that God had His hand on us and knew where He was taking us.

Don't believe the lie that your marriage was a mistake. God knows the plans He has for you and your husband and if you will trust your marriage to Him, it will work out. Yes, there will be difficult times, but take courage. Good marriages happen through hard work. You can't run away at the first sign of trouble. You may have different interests. There may be irritations and character traits that you don't like. But are you perfect? Many women want to divorce their husbands without making the effort to change, starting with themselves. Divorce is not the easy option it seems to be. Divorce leaves scars and brokenness. It is particularly hard on children.

Unless you have a valid reason, do your best to stay married and don't be selfish. Try and think back to what attracted you to your husband in the first place and look for the good in him.

Philippians 4:8 (Message Bible)

Summing it all up friends, I'd say you would do best by filling your minds and meditating on things true, noble, reputable, authentic, compelling, gracious, the best, not the worse, the beautiful, not the ugly; things to praise, not things to curse. Put into practice what you learned from me, what you heard and saw and realized. Do that, and God, who makes everything work together, will work you into His most excellent harmonies.

I love that last verse about excellent harmonies. Harmony is when voices blend together as one. Harmony in the home is when two people blend together as one, in spirit and in voice. There is power in agreement, so don't let the enemy deceive you with his lies. Stay united with your husband and you will experience the joy of a happy and peaceful marriage.

I've Fallen Out of Love with my Husband

I shared on the difference between love and lust in the first chapter on marriage and I trust you know the difference between the two. When someone comes to me and tells me they no longer love their husband and want a divorce, there are two questions I ask them.

Question 1: Do you believe God brought you and your husband together?

Question 2: Did you love your husband when you married him?

Take the time to think about what your answer would be. Love is not a feeling. Love goes much deeper than that, especially for the Christian. There are many times I don't feel love for my husband, and I am sure he could say the same of me! But love is not something you fall in and out of. The "in love" feeling when you first met does wear off. But that wasn't the real deal kind of love! Real love is unconditional and real love gives, regardless of feelings. Love your husband even when it hurts. Give your will over to the will of God, even when your spouse hurts you and you don't want to love him.

In marriage one must get beyond selfishness. Selfish love takes and withholds and does not regard the feelings of others. Selfish love uses and abuses. Real love never does. This feeling of not being in love is not a valid reason for divorce for the Christian. As a woman of God, I am commanded by Jesus to walk in love with all people, even my enemies. Now a non–believer would have a problem with this, because the God kind of love is not in them. But we should never have a problem with this love. It is something we need to work out daily in our lives. It starts in our home and carries through to everything else we are involved in.

You choose to love your husband. You walk it out in words and actions. Every day it will get easier and one day you will know that you truly do love your husband and you will be so thankful you never went through with that divorce.

There are other issues that I could write about concerning divorce, but the above are the most common ones. I want to close this chapter with the following thoughts.

Divorce goes right through families.

It is like a disease that will spread and contaminate down through the generations.

But thank God, there is a cure for it.

Determine to walk in the light of God's word. You can choose to follow God's plan for your marriage or not! Choose to please God and do what is right. By doing so, you are putting yourself on the path to blessing for you and your family. Don't let the devil destroy your life.

For those who are divorced, you also can choose to leave the past behind and remarry if you want to. Be free of condemnation and guilt and rise to a new and better life in the love of God and in the freedom of Christ Jesus.

The only ideal marriage is the one God sees for you and your spouse. Start to see things through the eyes of God and see what He will do.

2 Corinthians 4:18 (New King James Version)

While we do not look at the things which are seen, but at the things which are not seen.

For the things which are seen are temporary, but the things which are not seen are eternal.

15

The Mother

The pains were coming fast and furious as they wheeled her into the delivery room. She had longed for this day and had been preparing for the birth by attending all the pre–natal classes and reading all she could on pregnancy, birth and motherhood.

Motherhood.

Even saying it brought a sense of responsibility and commitment but there was also a nice warm feeling that came with that. She imagined cuddling her newborn baby and the feel of warm baby skin against her cheek. She hoped she would be able to breast feed and do the best she could to be a good mother.

Would she cope with a first baby? Would she be a good mother? Would she be able to keep her house tidy and her husband happy? He was very particular and liked everything to be organised and on time. She had taken pride in her home and had enjoyed planning menus and experimenting with different foods. They had discussed the changes that a baby would make to their lifestyle and had decided to take it step by step. They so badly wanted to be the best parents they could be.

The urge to push was so strong, but the midwife said to hold back. "Won't be long now dear, you're almost there!"

Her husband looked so nervous and his hand was white where she had gripped it so tightly during the contractions. She loved him so much. They were married nearly nine years. The first four years they had concentrated on getting to know each other and building a home. They both enjoyed travelling and every year chose somewhere different to go on holiday. They had so many interests in common and were both outdoor people. They loved to hike, mountain bike, and ski and go snowboarding. They wanted to be able to continue all these activities, so they had bought a backpack designed for carrying babies.

They had thought long and hard about having children. Both of them agreed that they wanted children and that now would be the right time to start. They thought that conception would be so easy, but as the years went by they began to get anxious and tried so hard to conceive. After seeking medical advice they were told that there was no physical reason why they couldn't have children. Maybe they were just too tense and stressed. The doctor suggested she take time out from her job and relax a bit more.

Three years went passed and when she missed her first period she nearly didn't notice it. It was her husband that asked her if she was OK when she had been feeling tired and was a bit pale. Only then did it dawn on her that she was two weeks late. When she got the confirmation that she was indeed pregnant, they had gone out and celebrated.

The months had flown in and both families were so excited about the baby. It would be the first grandchild on both sides of the family. What a special baby this would be. She pushed one last time and heard the cries of her son.

A beautiful boy! "Well done" said the midwife. There were no complications. It had not been a difficult birth. "I love you sweetheart. Thank you for our son." Her husband kissed her as she held their son for the first time.

Motherhood.

Was this love that welled up inside her for the helpless baby she held the fulfilment of being a woman? Had Eve felt this way when she had her first child? God had given them a wonderful gift. New life had been put into their care and with that came the awesome awareness of how they would have to provide, protect and train up this child. One day he would enter society and would contribute good things to the community he lives in. They couldn't make his choices for him but they could be there to guide him and encourage him by their words.

Psalm 127:2 (Message Bible)

Don't you see that children are God's best gifts, the fruit of the womb His generous legacy.

16

How to be a Godly Mother

You may never have been a mother before but being a mother is something you learn hands on! It is a bonus if you have been involved in helping with younger siblings at home, but not every woman has had the opportunity. Babies don't come with instruction manuals!

Babies do four things. They cry. They sleep. They eat. They fill nappies.

If you can learn to handle these four things then you will cope, but just remember, they also do these four things during the night! I never could understand how my husband, who was sleeping, could prod me in the side when the baby started crying. Wasn't he supposed to be sleeping?

Babies develop at different rates and some will talk before they can walk, or draw on the wall before they are potty trained.

Some Things Babies and Children Like To Do

* Drink water out of the fish bowl.

* Wipe sticky hands on a visitor's dress.

* Scream in the supermarket.

* Use the toilet on display in a DIY shop.

* Cough and sneeze without due care and attention.

* Learn to open child safety locks.

* Push the stop button on escalators.

* Jump on the bed.

* Identify medicine even when disguised in food or drink.

* Go organic, they eat mud.

* Stick marbles up their nose.

* Blow bubbles and eat soap.

* Only pooh in the bath when they share it with their siblings.

* Throw up in the car without warning.

* Empty waste paper bins.

* Leave half sucked lollipops on the furniture.

Don't you just love the little darlings?

Relax and enjoy them while they are little because they grow up so quickly, and before you know it, you have a teenager in the house! They also do four things.

They cry. They sleep. They eat. And they need a constant supply of money!

Motherhood

Woman is the life giving one and this can be summed up in one expression, motherhood. What a change we go through in our lives when we have our children. I was eighteen years old when our first son was born and I certainly was not equipped for being a mother. I wasn't a Christian then and had read no books that could have prepared me for what lay ahead. I am thankful for the help of my mother and mother–in–law and other women who input into my life at that time. I remember having so many questions about the sleeping and eating habits of babies. I worked through all the different stages; colic, teething, potty training and all the stuff that comes with babies and children, which was not easy.

Many women have now to be both mother and father to their children, which can be challenging. I had the support of my husband, which was so needed, especially as we brought up two boys. My heart goes out to single mothers and to those who have no support in their parenting for whatever reason.

We have a lot of single mothers and some single fathers in our church and we do all we can to be a support and lifeline to them. Fatherlessness is rife here in Scotland and it is the children who are suffering. My heart breaks for the young ones, who are being abused, neglected, deprived, made hopeless, starved of love and affection and who follow the ruinous road of substance and alcohol abuse which leads to destruction. May God help us to make the difference and to be part of the solution to turning young hearts back to the Father heart of God. Oh how they need the message of faith, hope and love that we as Christian women can give them.

Our church in Scotland is passionate about the future generations and has at heart the preservation of family values and love.

The reason my husband is passionate about men's ministry, is to raise up men that will take their place in the home, church, community and the nation. We need strong men in the times we live in and we are thankful for the difference we are seeing in the young men he is fathering.

We believe in mentoring young men and women and our mandate is that we decrease so that they can increase. We do this by inputting into their lives through teaching, books and by sharing our experiences. We want them to be the best parents they can be and by opening our lives to them and sharing our mistakes, they in turn, don't have to make the same mistakes we did.

There are certain elements mothers bring into the home so there can be completeness. Security, stability, strength of heart, gentleness, compassion, forbearance and longsuffering are only some of the attributes a mother needs to cultivate.

Things get out of balance when we get out of our intended purpose, and if you have children, then you have to be a mother on purpose!

It is the duty of parents to:

* Love
* Teach
* Train
* Control and correct
* Provide

There are so many self-help books on the subject of motherhood, but not all of them are based on God's word, which should be our manual for life. God created us, and only He knows best what we need.

As a minister and speaker at many women's conferences, I do share on parenting quite a lot and when I have question time, the women ask the same questions, no matter where they are from, be it Africa, USA, Europe, Australia. Mothers are looking for Godly wisdom on how they can successfully bring up their children. I will be sharing briefly on each of the five duties of parents and I pray that this will help you in the exciting adventure ahead!

LOVE

The love of God has to continually dwell in you and be worked out in you. Love is not an emotion but raising children can indeed be very emotional! There are times when your little blessing may push you to the limits, but love is patient, kind, forbearing and will go the extra mile. Let all you do for your child be motivated by love and not selfishness. Don't try and live out your unfulfilled dreams through your children, but rather cultivate the gifts and talents that God has given them and do your best not to be controlling about it.

Make sure that you and your husband demonstrate your affection for one another in front of your children. Let hugs and kisses be a normal part of their lives. Give your husband the reverence due to him and your children will do the same. Never argue in front of them or undermine a decision your husband has made in front of them. If you feel it was unfair, speak to your husband about it while the children are not there. They are quick to pick up on disagreement and where there is no agreement, you are toast!! Children absorb into their own personalities the behaviour learned in the home. It is not just what you do but who you are that speaks to a child. So love your children and teach them to love God.

Giving is what love is about. Actions and attitudes speak louder than words. Never talk down to or belittle your children. Let them know they are loved, equally.

Read *1 Corinthians 13* from the Amplified bible daily, in the first person. You can say, "I am patient and kind", and apply that love walk in all you do on a daily basis.

TEACH

The greatest way you can teach is by example.

Deuteronomy 6:6–7

And these words I command you this day shall be in your heart. You shall teach them diligently to your children and shall talk of them when you sit in your home, when you walk by the way, when you lie down, and when you rise up.

In other words, teaching your children about God, who He is and about His word, is a total lifestyle. It is wonderful to belong to a great church with a strong children's ministry, but you cannot lay down the responsibility of teaching your children and then blame the church, or the schools when they don't turn out the way you wanted them to. Yes mother, you do have authority over your children, but with that comes responsibility.

We celebrated our 40th wedding anniversary in 2007 and our children reiterated what they said about us at our 25th anniversary. They all said the same thing about us and that was, we were, are, and always will be consistent! Responsibility is consistence. It's being the same no matter how and what you feel. In the times we live in, your children need you to teach them about God, His word, honour in the home, core values and how to respect the world they live in.

TRAIN

To train is to put action to what you teach your children. They will in turn get wisdom from the knowledge they have, as they put that knowledge into practice. Training involves a lot of correcting.

Proverbs 22:6 (Message Bible)

Train up a child in the way he should go. And when he is old he will not depart from it. Point your kids in the right direction and when they are old they won't be lost.

Children need guidance; otherwise they will do whatever they want. How do you make children do what they don't want to and how do you make them do what God's word says? The way to do this is by patiently training the child to walk and live in the word. Training children is a lot harder on the parent than on the child. There are times when there could be a battle of wills. You may end up in tears. You may want to give up and give in to the child just to get some peace! Don't do it. Keep on keeping on! Training requires practice. Don't let your children or other people deceive you into thinking that you are putting pressure on your children. In other words, don't let your child intimidate you. Intimidation is when someone takes your authority away from you and then uses it against you and children are great at that.

A sports coach tells his team what to do and the team respect him. So it should be for you. You can look at out of control adults and see that they have had no training when they were young. It is a lot easier to deal with an out of control child than a teen or an adult. If children aren't controlled, they could hurt themselves or others.

Our daughter has a points system as part of her training for our grandchildren. Points mean prizes! She has found that this reward system works very well, but only if it is applied consistently.

Training will cost you. You need to know what to do before you pass that on to your children. You may have to read books or ask questions, but you need to know the way in order to point the way.

1 Timothy 3:4

One who rules his house well, having his children in submission with all reverence.

The Greek meaning in this verse for the word rule is to stand up in front and lead by example.

Proverbs 20:7 (Message Bible)

Good loyal people living honest lives make it much easier for their children.

If anything is ruling over you then that controls you. Make sure you are not an out of control mother. Don't lose your temper. Make sure your home is a place of peace, not war! Don't let your children embarrass you by being destructive, disruptive, and disrespectful or destroy other people's property. Remember, the training starts in the home. Train them to respect the value of things in your home and then they won't dishonour other people's homes or possessions.

CONTROL & CORRECT

Children are like young trees; you can bend them the way they are supposed to grow.

Proverbs 13:24

He who loves his child disciplines him promptly.

The earlier you start correcting your child the better. Proverbs is full of scriptures pertaining to parenting. It is one of my favourite books and I read it a lot. I find it very practical and I get wisdom and instruction for so many of the day-to-day things I have to deal with.

Many of the scriptures that deal with discipline refer to the rod of correction. A rod was a reed like stick, and was a sign of authority delegated from God to man. It was also used to lean on, lead and pull back from danger, like a shepherd's crook.

Psalm 23 is a wonderful description of the love and care a shepherd has for his sheep.

Ephesians 6:4

And you fathers, do not provoke your children to wrath, but bring them up in the training and admonition of the Lord.

Don't provoke your children. When parents give out undeserved correction or are harsh in their discipline then they are provoking their children to anger. There are so many angry, sullen children because of abusive parents.

Proverbs 19:18

Chasten your son while there is hope, and do not set your heart on his destruction. If you don't, you will ruin his life. (Living Bible)

Don't wait until it is too late. There is a time it could become hopeless. Don't let their tears intimidate you. It is hard, but you have to ignore their tears and do what you know to be right. Chasten means to reform, instruct, reprove and teach. Our Father God loves us and He chastens us.

Hebrews 12:6

Those whom the Lord loves, He chastens.

Always remember, a child is the product of what he or she is taught in the home.

Proverbs 19:18

Discipline your children while you still have the chance, indulging them will destroy them.

Don't spoil your children.

Be flexible without compromising. If you are not flexible you can break the spirit of a child and that is not good. I find that children respond to love and boundaries that are based on God's word and that are fair. Fairness and firmness is what a mother must stand for.

Dictatorship is not discipline. If you shout at your children and beat your children then you are the one that is out of control, not them. You may get them to do what you want out of fear, but you won't have their love or their respect. Force is not discipline. You have to rule with wisdom and love. You have to correct your child when they wilfully disobey you. You are the authority in the home, not them.

Proverbs 23:13–14

Don't be afraid to correct your young ones, a spanking wont kill them.

A good spanking (Not hard beating!) *in fact might save them from something worse than death.*

Proverbs 20:30

Strokes for correction reach to the innermost part.

Discipline with Balance

If your child is rebellious, they need to be touched and changed from their spirit, their innermost part. Parents should discipline their children according to and in line with God's word.

I made plenty of mistakes when it came to disciplining our children, but thankfully I have learned from those mistakes. I do give advice when asked and this is based on what I have learned through the years.

You cannot, not discipline your children, but do not be harsh with them. They are not being punished, but corrected. Be consistent, be firm and always let them know you love them, just like God does with you!

I don't believe it's right to spank a child for making a mistake or having an accident, like spilling a drink or making a mess, or breaking something. But if a child is deliberately destructive then the parents should discipline the child. How you do this is your choice, but make sure you and your spouse are in agreement as to what form the discipline should be.

If a child is knowingly disrespectful, cheeky, or rebellious, then he or she should be disciplined. It all culminates in the heart attitude of the child. An unthankful, surly child grieves a parent's heart and brings shame to the family. A thankful, joyful child is like a ray of sunlight on a cloudy day and brings laughter and peace into the heart of a parent.

If your child is moody, uncommunicative and miserable, then you have to take the time to talk with them and find out the reason for their behaviour. Perhaps they are being bullied at school, or they are worried about something. Do what you can to dispel their fears and let them know they are loved and you will see a difference in them. But they also need to know that you have boundaries set down for them and they will pay the consequences for breaching those boundaries.

In disciplining our children, I learned when to be flexible without compromising. For example, we had a time set out for when our daughter had to be home for, but we bent the rule when it was a special occasion. She respected this and never abused it, or us!

Use wisdom and learn to be flexible and you will have happy and contented children. You will get to the place where you don't have to correct your children as frequently and you can really delight yourself in your child and not dread having to take them any place in case they embarrass you.

Proverbs 29:17

Correct your son and he will give you rest, yes; he will give delight to your heart.

Peace is the key to success as a mother. May God grant you His wisdom for all the decisions you need to make as a mother, and may you always be led by His peace.

PROVIDE

2 Corinthians 12:14

For the children ought not to lay up for the parents, but the parents for the children.

We provide material things for our children, as well as the intangible. We have to provide food. This should be good, wholesome and nutritious. Don't give your children food that will cause them to develop bad eating habits and obesity. If you are not the best cook, then get a cookbook or download simple and easy recipes from the web. You don't have to spend a fortune on food either. You spend more on fast food and convenience food that is mostly poor in nutrition, than you would on fresh food. Making a meal from scratch, using good, wholesome food does not only cost less, but it can also be prepared in less than half an hour. You have to provide nutritious meals. Use wisdom in this by providing a variety of food. Don't force your child to eat food he doesn't like. Start when they are still young to develop and teach self–control and good, healthy eating habits. Fat kills in more ways than one.

You also have to provide clothing – not rags so your children are ashamed, but it doesn't have to be expensive, designer labels either. There are some great shops that offer good, quality fashion for children. You don't have to break the bank or get into debt clothing your children. Dress them modestly and warmly and help them to appreciate the value of taking care of their "stuff".

I take my grandchildren shopping for their summer and winter outfits. When it's the girls we have a "here comes the girls" day out which includes a meal. We have such a good time and they so enjoy going around the shop filling a basket. They try on the clothes and I get them to choose what they really want according to my budget.

It's the same with the boys. Only they usually take less time! I don't take them to the expensive shops but I get them trendy gear which will last at least for a season. Children outgrow their clothes so quickly, which is another reason for not overspending on outfits.

Another important task is to teach them about hygiene. Washing themselves and brushing their teeth is a good idea! These things should become good habits and shouldn't be regarded as a chore.

Provide the comfort of a home where they can come into an atmosphere of security, love and a safe haven, where they can express themselves and still be accepted. Don't set them up for ridicule or let your home be a place of ridicule. Don't use your children as objects of derision or allow anyone else to. Keep slating remarks and sarcasm out of your home. Have an open forum where they can be encouraged to be creative. Let them know you appreciate their input and always give them your full attention when they speak to you. But they also shouldn't be allowed to express rebellion.

Communication is the basis for any good strong relationship and that works two ways. Don't assume your children know what you require of them. You have to let them know your expectations or you are setting yourself and them up for disappointment. Talk and listen, but do more listening than talking. If you don't have their ear, then who does? You may not like it when you find out, so make sure they can come to you about anything, however big or small. Provide that listening ear.

We all want our children to have it better than we did, but making things too easy for them is also not good. It does not teach them the value of things and they need to see that work provides the finances they need. Always point them to God as their source and not you. Teach them to tithe as soon as they are old enough to understand it. This will create in them the desire to honour God and it will encourage them to exercise faith in Him as their provider. Teach them to save. Open a savings account in their name so they learn that money is not just to be spent the moment they have any. It will help them to understand that they also can contribute towards the things they want to have and for holidays etc.

Make provision for their education. Help them with their giftings and talents, but at their own level. Help them to develop their self worth by praising and affirming them. Don't plant seeds of self–rejection by constantly nagging or ridiculing them about their faults or weaknesses. Watch your words. Don't confuse who the child is, with what the child does! Children sense they are really loved by the actions of the parents towards them and by the atmosphere in the home. As a mother you have the responsibility to have peace ruling in your home.

Do your best to facilitate their talents. Our one grandson is so gifted in music and wants to make that his career. To get the best possible tuition for him, his parents are prepared to make whatever sacrifices they can. It means they have to finance his tuition and transport him to all the classes he has. They work with us in ministry at the church and lead a full life but they want to know they are doing the best they can to give him a platform for his talent to be seen and heard. It could be your child is gifted in sports, art, writing, cooking, building or whatever. Do your best for them, that is all that is required from a parent. Do what you can and trust God to do what you can't.

Our oldest grandson graduates from four years at bible school in Accra, Ghana. That was a tough one for all of us as a family. We miss him and he only gets home for Christmas, but he is doing what he wants to do. We have to release our children into their destiny no matter how difficult it may be for us. He has matured so much and has learned responsibility as well as how to adapt to a new culture. How many young people get the opportunity to travel at such a young age? As parents, we need to cast the care of our children onto God. He can take better care of them than we can and He knows their end from their beginning. Your child has a destiny, so help them achieve their goals and don't interfere with God's purpose for them.

Our one grandson wants to be a vet so we will do the best we can for him. Two of our granddaughters enjoy dancing, and the youngest enjoys drama.

Don't compare your children with each other or with other children. This leads to low self-esteem, which can be hard to recover from. They are all different and all unique, and we need to recognise that and celebrate their differences.

Did you know that here in the UK there are an estimated 15,000 under 18's currently on antidepressants? Alcohol, drugs, family conflicts and breakdown are the cause of many child suicides. The price of privilege that children pay whose parents earn more than £60,000 a year, have three times the rate of depression and anxiety disorders as ordinary teenagers. The organisation, NICE, officially advocated the prescription of Prozac (flouxetine) for children aged eight and above. Many of them are prescribed these antidepressants without receiving psychological support.

They made the following statement:

The best treatment is psychological therapy as well as therapy for the whole family, so they can better understand and learn how to support the child who is suffering.

These statistics may shock you, but maybe that's what it will take for things to change. Mothers, it is time to be who you were created to be, the life giving one.

Don't Worry About Your Children

My husband and I love to input into the lives of the young men and women in our church. It is so important to pass on what we have learned in our many years of marriage. Having brought up three children with eight grandchildren, we have put a lot of time and prayer energy into being parents. On reflection, we have made some mistakes, but we thank God for His help. We did the best we knew how and were diligent in teaching and training up our children.

Our children are grown up now and have to train up their children. They have to make their own choices and be responsible to God for them. If you have made mistakes in the past and you have asked forgiveness, you must move on. You can't blame yourself for the wrong choices your children may make. It is not your fault when your children make wrong choices. We cannot think for them or control them; we simply have to release them into God's care. If you have done the best you could, then so what if you blew it at times. If you, like me, are genuinely sorry and did your best, then you have to go forward. Look back in fondness on the good times and pass on your experience of what you learnt. Don't interfere, but if you are asked for advice, then offer what you can.

God is doing a renewing, transforming work in our minds, as we put His word in there. Look on it as reprogramming. Get rid of guilt and self-condemnation. Enjoy where you are in your life right now. When our children make mistakes, it is hard for us to see them work through the consequences, but you have to let them do that. Trying to "soften" everything for them will not help. Be led by God on what to do for them and don't interfere. If they know you are there for them if and when needed, then that is enough.

17

The Woman in Debt

She woke up and peeked out the window. It was bright and sunny with frost on the ground. She would go for a walk in the country today. She loved the wee village she lived in and the beautiful walks all around the open countryside. The people were so friendly and it was a great place to bring up their two children, a boy of ten and a girl of seven. Her husband commuted to his work in the city where he worked as an accountant for a big publishing company. He earned a good salary but it seemed to get swallowed up with the mortgage, car, travelling expenses and the day to day household expenses for a family of four.

She didn't want to think about money, or the lack of it, right now. Her husband left the house at six in the morning except weekends. She would sleep on till quarter to eight and then get the children up for breakfast. After that they would leave for school, which was just around the corner, so there was no need to go with them. She had the use of their new red people carrier. They enjoyed the space it afforded them when they went out for a drive. The running costs on it were high, but they needed something to get around in at weekends.

She was just about to leave for her walk when she saw the postman delivering letters. The fear rose up in her. The familiar brown envelopes were lying on her hallway floor. She didn't want to open them, but she might as well do it now rather than later. It made no difference.

Final Reminders, Legal Action. It was all that filled her thoughts, waking and sleeping. There was no respite from the bondage of debt she had got herself into.

It had started two years ago, when they had bought the house. They knew they were stretching their commitments with the larger mortgage but were willing to tighten their belt and cut down on other less important things. They had agreed that it would be worth the sacrifice for the better quality of life they would have in the village. Her husband was due a promotion and that would bring in a salary increase, but that had not happened. The company had actually had cutbacks and he was thankful not to have been made redundant.

She had looked for part time work. With her secretarial experience she thought it would have been easy but there was nothing in the village. She could get work in the city but it would mean working full time and with the travelling time involved, the children would need to go into after school care, which was expensive. Then there were school holidays, which would mean full time care. It wasn't worth it and she really wanted to be there for the children. Most of the village folk were prosperous and they enjoyed a high standard of living. Many of them had their own businesses and some worked from home. They had a good social life, which revolved around the community. Everybody knew one another and there was a certain snobbishness and pride, which permeated through the village.

She had to get the children new sports equipment for all their different after school activities; rugby, basketball, ballet and music lessons. She had ordered what they needed from a catalogue. If she cut down on groceries, she could pay the monthly amount due. Her son also wanted to take guitar lessons. She had been looking for a good, second hand guitar but he wanted a new one and then there was the weekly cost of the lessons. She felt guilty having to say no to him. Why should he do without when all the other children were able to have lessons? She didn't know whether he had musical talent but she wanted him to have every opportunity that life afforded him, so she had gone ahead and got him the new guitar and all that came with it.

Christmas had just passed and that had meant more purchases on the credit card. Gifts for the family, a new dress for the work's dance and all the food and drink they needed to host friends throughout the Christmas season. She didn't think about the rising interest she was incurring and she didn't stop spending.

Even when she didn't really need to shop, she found herself ordering from catalogues and TV shopping channels. It was so easy. Just call them and give them the credit card details. They never asked if you had debt, in fact, it was easier if you already had a credit rating.

Her husband was so busy working he didn't always notice the new clothes, toys and home wares. She had hidden many of her purchases in a cupboard under the stairs. Many of them were still in their boxes having never been opened. That wasn't all she had hidden. The final demands from her creditors were torn up and put in the bucket.

She was sick to her stomach. What could she do?

She had thought the fresh air would help her feel better but when she walked through her front door after her walk, she felt as though she was walking into a prison. How could she feel that about her lovely home?

She had called all the debt consolidators she could find in the phone book, but none of them could help her because she and her husband had a joint mortgage and she needed his permission and signature before she could do anything. That would mean confessing the debt to him and she could never do that. He hated debt and wouldn't understand how she had got into it so deep. More important, would he forgive her for lying to him and deceiving him?

Oh God, what a mess!

She had been issued with a sheriff's writ, and the bailiffs were due at the house tomorrow. She would go out and they would have to go away. She was sure they wouldn't enter the house by force and she needed more time to think. She had been robbing Peter to pay Paul! It was like a game to her. Whoever put on the most pressure got paid, but she couldn't keep up the juggling act anymore. She also couldn't keep up the pretence that all was well. She would die of shame if any of her friends and neighbours found out how much in debt she was. It was important for the children that their family be accepted as part of the village culture.

She sat down and cried. She couldn't go on like this. She could call the citizen's advice lifeline and get help, but they would want her to tell her husband. She had read somewhere that compulsive shopping was a sickness. That was rubbish. She knew she could stop whenever she wanted. If you needed something, you bought it. It was that simple. People who gambled or drank too much had problems, but not her. These help lines were for weak people, not for her.

She switched on the TV and it came on to the shopping channel. She had better hit the off button. They were advertising new exercise equipment. She had been putting on a bit of weight lately. She really needed something like that to help her get fit, and maybe, if her husband saw her slim again, he will see that it was worth it.

Now where did she put that credit card?

18

Wisdom in Finances

I was brought up in a home where everything was paid for with, or by cash. If my parents couldn't afford it, we didn't get it. It was that simple. If we really wanted something bad enough, we had to save up for it and wait till we had the cash to buy it.

This taught me patience and gave me a good foundation as far as overspending was concerned. I carried this into my own marriage and always did my best to live within our means. As a young wife and mother, I did not have the knowledge of God's Word to help me see Him as my provider, but I did have the understanding that getting into debt was not an option. We built our marriage and our home a bit at a time and although we didn't have a lot when we started, we worked together to furnish our home and provide for our children. We taught them that they couldn't get everything they set their eyes on and to appreciate and look after what they did have.

Many young couples today are not prepared to wait until they have the cash to furnish their home and want everything now! This puts pressure on their finances and on their relationship and they miss out of the joy of laying a good solid foundation, which can be built upon and which will never crumble and fall.

By going into debt to buy things, you are not giving God the opportunity to act on your behalf by opening up avenues of provision for you and your family. Children especially need to be taught to see God as their provider and they should be encouraged to tithe and to save. I love to take our grandchildren shopping, but I always point out to them that it is because of God's provision and faith in His word that I am able to bless them.

I enjoy Dickens and one of my favourite novels is *David Copperfield*. There is a character in the story called Mr McCorber. He had the unfortunate experience of finding himself in prison for debt and he passed on the following words of wisdom to young *David Copperfield*.

Annual income twenty pounds, annual expenditure nineteen pounds nineteen shillings and sixpence, bliss.

Annual income twenty pounds, annual expenditure Twenty pounds and sixpence, misery!

The bottom line is, if your outgoings are more than your incomings, then your shortfall will be your downfall!

That may not be proper English, but it does get the message across – Stay out of Debt!

We serve a generous God who wants to show Himself strong on our behalf.

2 Chronicles 16:9

For the eyes of the Lord run to and fro throughout the whole earth to show Himself strong on behalf of those whose hearts are blameless towards Him.

He wants people to notice that we are blessed so that we can share with them the goodness of God. My husband and I have a mandate to take the Gospel to the nation of Scotland and beyond.

Until everyone is saved, we will preach the salvation of the Lord. Until everyone is healed, we will preach the healing power of Jesus. Until everyone is free from the bondage of debt, the church has to share the message that God is their source and provider.

Many Christians are ignorant of this and that is the reason they cannot exercise their faith in God in the area of their finances.

Prosperity is not the state of having, but the continual expectation of increase. So that whatever you have, you are free to give.

Poverty is not the state of not having, but the fear of not getting more. There is no expectation of increase, so that you hold on to whatever you have.

Proverbs 11:24 & 25.

It is possible to give away and become richer. It is also possible to hold on too tightly and lose everything.

The bible says money answers all things!

Ecclesiastes 10:19

A feast was made for laughter and wine makes merry but money answers everything.

It would look that way, especially when you are broke. But money, without the wisdom to handle it, can get people into trouble. You can make wrong investments and end up in debt.

My husband and I used to have our own business and I remember a time when there was a recession and we had no income for nearly a year. We did the best we could and tightened our belt, but we had to depend on the bank to help us. Of course banks will help, but not without it costing you a large amount of interest. We thank God for His provision during that time and for answered prayer and the wisdom to get through a difficult situation, but without God, I don't know how we would have made it. We have always believed that God wants to bless His children and that as long as we obeyed Him in tithing and seeking first His Kingdom, all the other things would come right in our lives. We have found this to be so.

What does God think of poverty? Do you have to be poor to be Godly? Does God want you to be in debt?

Proverbs 10:15

The rich man's wealth is his strong city; the poverty of the poor is their ruin.

Verse 22 *The blessing of the Lord, it makes rich, and He adds no sorrow with it.*

Prosperity is an obedience message. If you obey, you will receive.

In our church we have qualified and professional people who can advise people and help them get out of debt. The statistics of people who are in debt here in Scotland are very high. More and more people are overspending on their credit cards and this is increasing due to the aggressive marketing of the finance companies. Sadly, many young men and women are getting into the debt trap, and many of them already owe thousands of pounds because of student loans.

When our sons went to college, we encouraged them to get part time work to help supplement the income we supplied them with. This built into them a good solid work ethic. Many young people don't seek work and rely on the government for their income, and this is something that needs to be addressed and confronted. As we share the Gospel and teach life principles, we are seeing lives changed and many young people applying themselves to study and to seeking employment. My husband loves to share entrepreneurial skills with young people and already some have opened up their own businesses and are looking at creative ways to prosper the Kingdom of God here in Scotland.

You can get something out of nothing! Ask God to give you the ideas and the strategy and then apply your faith in Him for the right connections and appointments you need. God always works though people. Right associations will bring increase into your life.

You may be in a heap of trouble and in debt right now, but it is never too late to change and you can get help, if you want it! Debt has power over us when we try and hide it and pretend that it doesn't exist. Be open and honest, especially with your husband and get into agreement on the best way forward.

Here are some things you can do which will make a start to breaking the bondage of debt:

1. Tithe

The purpose of tithing is to teach you to always put God first in your life. You can't afford not to tithe.

Proverbs 3:9–10

Honour the Lord with your capital and sufficiency from righteous labours and with the first fruits of all your income.

So shall your storage places be filled with plenty and your vats with new wine?

2. God is your Provider.

Philippians 4:19 (Hudson)

And my God, on the scale of His wealth, will fully supply in Christ Jesus, your every need.

3. Ask God for ways to Prosper

Deuteronomy 8:18

But you shall remember the Lord your God, for it is He who gives you the power to get wealth that He may establish His covenant forever.

4. Declare and call your harvest in.

Proverbs 18:20

You eat the fruit of your mouth.

A man's self shall be filled with the fruit of his mouth and with the consequence of his words he must be satisfied, whether good or bad.

You have to put your mouth to work by speaking God's word and provision over your life, family, work and business.

5. Determine to get out of Debt

There are many scriptures in Proverbs that warn us to stay out of debt and not to stand surety for anyone.

Proverbs 6:1–5

My son, if you become surety for your friend. If you have shaken hands in pledge for a stranger, you are snared by the words of your own mouth, you are taken by the words of your mouth. So do this, my son, and deliver yourself, for you have come into the hand of your friend, go and humble yourself, Plead with your friend, give no sleep to your eyes, nor slumber to your eyelids. Deliver yourself like a gazelle from the hand of the hunter, and like a bird from the hand of the fowler.

Proverbs 17:18

A man devoid of understanding shakes hands in a pledge, and becomes surety for his friend.

Proverbs 20:16

Take the garment of one, who is surety for a stranger, and hold it as a pledge when it is for a seductress.

It's hard to say no to family and friends, but being a guarantor is a sure way to destroy good relationships. I would rather give to someone who needs help, than give a loan or pledge surety for his or her borrowing. Use wisdom when it comes to finances and you will not live with regrets.

The devil robs people through holding them in the bondage of debt. Attack your debt and get help. Stop spending and stop charging on your accounts and credit cards. Cut up your credit cards and throw away your catalogues. Don't tune into the shopping channels on T.V. Do whatever it takes. Bite the bullet! Chew on the leather! But get free!

6. Give Offerings

Luke 6:38 (New Living Translation)

You will get in exactly the same proportion as you give.

Matthew 6:33 (Phillips)

Set your heart on His Kingdom and His goodness, and all these things will come to you as a matter of course.

All what things? The answer is, the things that concern you. Once you realise that God is interested in your welfare and every area of your life, you will have confidence in His provision, protection and care. If He can take good care of the birds and the flowers, then He can certainly take good care of you.

If you are in debt and are feeling overwhelmed, my prayer for you is that God will strengthen you, guide you and connect you with the people who can help you get free.

In God, you can do all things. It is not impossible when your trust is in Him.

19

The Menopausal Woman

She froze as she stood at the top of the escalator. She was sweating and her heart was pumping too fast. Her breath began to come in short gasps and she could not control the overwhelming panic that came upon her. Two teenagers were coming up on the escalator next to her and were staring at her. They began to laugh at her. "Silly old bird", she heard one of them saying. Was fifty–one old?

A young couple came up behind her but she couldn't move to let them past. It was as if she was frozen to the spot in panic and fear. The young woman put her arm around her, "Are you all right?" The question came with genuine concern in her voice. The young woman took her by the arm and led her away from the top of the escalator and to the nearest sales counter, where one of the assistants found her a chair and brought her a glass of water. She was breathing more evenly now and crying softly.

'I'm sorry". She began to apologise to everyone around her. "No problem", said the sales assistant. "Just take your time and I'll take you down on the lift. Do you have transport to get home?" "I have my car" she replied shakily. She began to dig in her handbag for the car keys, but could not find them. Her husband was always getting irritated with her for not being able to find things. "Stupid woman", he would shout at her. Where were her keys? What if she had left them in the car and someone had stolen it! Or maybe they had fallen out of her bag when she paid for her last purchase! As she began to empty the bag, panic rose up in her once again.

'I've lost my keys!" she said. The assistant took the bag from her gently, "Let me help you dear". The sales assistant was very patient and kind to her. This made her want to cry even more. When was the last time someone had been gentle with her? When was the last time she had been shown any consideration or affection?

"I've found them. They were in the mirror pocket of your bag. Oh I've done the same myself. I put things away so I can get my hands on them easily and then forget where I put them!" She remembered now, she had put them there so it would be easy to find them.

As she drove home her mind went over the events of the day. She was stupid, a silly old bird, just like her husband was always telling her, same as the teenagers said. "You're neurotic and stupid". How many times a day had her husband said this to her? She had heard it so often; she believed it to be true.

He was always comparing her with the women he worked with at his office. They were well groomed, poised and competent. They had it together, and she didn't! Anxiety rose up in her as her mind conjured up pictures of her husband with his secretary. What if he said he was leaving her? What would she do? The only subject she did well in at school was art.

She had a flare for creativity, but had to leave school when she was fifteen to help with the income at home. She had good parents who loved her, but they had never encouraged her to follow through with her art. "Girls don't need a career", they had said. "Get a good man, have children and get on with it!" Was that a woman's lot? Pro–creation, be fruitful, multiply. Isn't that what the bible said?

Well, she had done her bit. She had five children, three boys and two girls. She had been eighteen when she had her first and twenty–seven when the fifth was born. She had been sterilised after that because of complications during childbirth. She thought back to that time. It had been so difficult. She was weak and sore after the surgery and her new baby daughter had been a restless and colicky child. She had no help from anyone when she got home from hospital and simply had to roll up her sleeves and get on with it. Her husband didn't believe it was a man's place to help with the housework or with the children. At that time they had moved because the company her husband worked with had transferred him to a new factory in another part of the country. She had never been good at making friends and there was no family there to help her. Her husband resented having to take time off work to look after the children while she had the baby and he couldn't wait to get back to work the day after she had arrived home. How had she got through that time?

The children were grown up now. Three were married and she had four grandchildren she loved very much. She took joy in their visits, but the lifestyle of the young parents now seemed to be so full and they really didn't have much time for visiting. Sometimes the only time she heard from them was when they needed a babysitter.

Of the other two, one had left home to live in Australia with friends, and then there was her youngest son. He was a drug addict. She worried about him so much. She didn't even know where he was. He had lied to her and stolen from her. He blamed his father for everything. He said he was picked on and nobody cared for him.... She did.

Where had she gone wrong? It was her fault. Wasn't it the mother who looked after the children and taught them right from wrong? What if he went to prison and killed himself. How would she live with the guilt? She thought about her daughter and son in law with the two children. He had lost his job last week. Had they enough to live on? They had just bought their first house. Perhaps she could look after the children and her daughter could go back to work? Yes, she would call and offer her help.

Her mind was full of thoughts as she pulled the car into the driveway. She looked around and noticed a police car parked outside her house. Oh God! Something terrible has happened! Was it her son? The fear and panic once again rose inside her. She got out of the car and let herself into the house. She looked out of the window. Thank God. They were just having lunch.

She sat down with her head in her hands and began to cry. Where were the pills the doctor had given her? She found them in the kitchen. She had hidden them there, as she didn't want her husband to know that she was taking them. He already thought she was a basket case. She had tried to communicate with him on how she was feeling, but he didn't want to listen. "Don't use the menopause as an excuse", he had said to her. "Other women cope with it and live normal lives. You're just neurotic. It runs in your family". He would get angry and start shouting and berating her. He had been verbally abusing her for years and she had never had the courage to stand up to him.

The pills helped calm her down and took that horrible knot away from her stomach. They did make her a bit drowsy, but she needed a sleep during the day because she couldn't shut her mind down at night. She was so tired all the time because she couldn't get to sleep and when she eventually get to sleep, she was woken up by night sweats.

She remembered the whispered conversations between her mother and her aunt. They would refer to women "going through the change of life". She now knew they were talking about the menopause.

Meno – pause...

Change of life was a better name for what she was experiencing! The hot flushes, the night sweats, the mood swings, the vaginal dryness and the lack of desire for lovemaking. But for her, the most difficult of all, was the feeling of inadequacy and fear. She had been having panic attacks almost daily and sometimes the fear and anxiety became more than she could bear.

She would stay at home. She didn't want to go out and face people. Better to stay at home. Better to switch off. The pills helped her do that, although she did need to take two now instead of one, to get the same result. She must remember to get a repeat prescription. She couldn't live without the pills. Life was hopeless without them.

Did all women feel like her, fearful, worthless and stupid? Was her life over now that the children had left home? She had fulfilled her purpose as a woman, so what was left? What could take away the fear and worry? She was a lousy wife and mother. She felt guilty all the time. Where could she find peace? She was convinced she was to blame for everything bad that had happened to her and her family.

If only she could get a new mindset that thought on the good and not on the bad things. Maybe she needed to talk to someone. She picked up the flyer from the church down the street. It had come through the door just last week.

"Feeling down in the dumps, depressed? We can help you. Ladies group starting next Wednesday. Call for details."

She picked up the phone and dialled the number....

20

Understanding the Process of Menopause

Some of the many symptoms of menopause are insecurity, anxiety and mood swings.

So many women battle in the area of their minds. They are fearful and anxious. Worry and all that comes with it becomes a way of life to them.

Because of all the hormonal mood swings women have during menopause, it is important to make sure you have a healthy mind. To do this you need to renew your mind with the word of God. That means taking the scriptures in the bible and applying them to your life through speaking them out and living it out in practise.

The saying goes "You die if you worry, and you die if you don't!" Not so!

You die quicker if you allow worry and anxiety to rule in your mind.

Your fear attracts the wrong thing and very often, the very thing you are afraid of! But, faith repels it.

Ephesians 6:16

Lift up over all the covering shield of faith upon which you can quench all the flaming missiles of the wicked one.

Fear is the opposite of faith and does not originate from God. Fear is born out of toxic thoughts. You can't stop thoughts from coming to you, but you don't have to dwell on them.

2 Timothy 1:7

For God did not give us a spirit of fear, but power, love and a sound (normal) mind.

If you are a follower of God, you don't have to put up with thoughts of fear and doubt. You can choose to think on positive things such as scriptures, which tell you who you are in Christ.

Your mind is a battleground and the enemy will try and get you caught up in the negative thoughts he puts there, but God has given you weapons to use against him.

You can pray in the name of Jesus. You can plead the blood of Jesus. You can speak the word of God into every situation.

Take every thought captive to the obedience of Christ. Any thought that is contrary to the word of God, is not from God.

2 Corinthians 10:4 (Amplified Bible)

For the weapons of our warfare are not physical weapons of flesh and blood, but they are mighty before God for the overthrow and destruction of strongholds. In as much as we refute arguments and theories and reasoning's and every proud and lofty thing that sets itself up against the true knowledge of God, and we lead every thought and purpose away captive into the obedience of Christ.

Fear causes stress and stress causes sickness and disease. Medical science has proven that many illnesses are stress related.

Sickness is a physical manifestation of stress. Statistics tell us that more and more people are on prescription drugs for anxiety and depression. The pills cannot cure the root of depression and are in themselves often addictive. Many times fear and worry are deep-rooted family traits that need to be expelled once and for all. We do this by choosing not to give these negative thoughts and fears any place in our mind.

My family had some traits that were not good and I had to make a decision that I was not going down that route of worry, anxiety, panic or fear. It stopped with me! There was no way I would give in to those emotions, nor would they be passed on to our children. I prayed against these things in the name of Jesus and whenever any of those disabling thoughts would come into my mind, I would deal with them immediately. If I didn't deal with them quickly, it wasn't long before my mind took me where I didn't want to go. I learned to replace the negative, disabling thoughts with positive, uplifting thoughts. I had to renew my mind with God's word.

Romans 12:2

Don't be conformed to this world but be transformed by the renewing of your mind.

It's like rebooting a computer. You have to get rid of the old stinking thinking, and reprogram your mind to thinking based on who God says you are in Christ. Jesus said that from the abundance of the heart, the mouth speaks. Whatever you think will eventually come out of your mouth.

Are you a negative, fretful, anxious person or are you positive, sure and calm? You will know where you are at if you have peace in your life. I read scriptures on the peace of God and focussed on that. You see, because I have Jesus living on the inside of me, I have peace on the inside of me, because Jesus is the Prince of Peace. Peace guards my heart and my mind.

Colossians 3:15

And let the peace of God rule in your hearts, to which you were also called in one body and be thankful.

Either peace rules or worry rules. I chose to let peace rule. Life is not about chance, but about choice! We live with the choices we make.

Menopause

As women, we do have hormonal changes which can cause fear and insecurity, but only if we allow it. We can choose not to allow it. Working through menopause was a walk of faith for me. I could write a book on that subject alone! I could have given into fear, depression, mood swings and all the "stuff" associated with that, but I made a decision that I was going to the "other side", sane and in one piece!

After talking to other women about some of the things that my husband thought I was the only woman doing, I learned that I wasn't. It is a 'woman' thing. We don't like our man to drive too fast! We say "watch!" when we think he is too near the car in front! We like to get to the airport in plenty of time! We all dig for stuff in our handbags! We like to make lists! We do like to make sure everything is switched off and the door is locked when we go out of the house. And we ask our husband, every night has he put all the lights off and locked the door. We may repeat ourselves! Need I go on!!

But, that is no excuse!

There are some things we can do which will help us get through menopause. Doctor Reginald B. Cherry has written a book called 'God's Pathway to Healing Menopause'. He lists some of the natural plant extracts and supplements we can take which will not only alleviate the symptoms but also aid healing and strength in other areas. I do take mineral and vitamin supplements and find that they have helped boost my immune system and have benefited me in other areas. There are supplements especially formulated for women going through menopause. You can get advice from your local health food store on what will be best for you.

Diet and exercise also play a part in our overall well -being.

I like to run and do my best to get out two or three times a week. It keeps me fit and helps clear my mind as well as getting some fresh air. There are many different types of exercise we can do and walking and swimming are two of the best that I enjoy. I also do weights for my upper body, which helps with bone density. Many older women suffer from brittle bone disease, but there are positive things we can do to stop the progression and many times stop it from happening. This of course, takes a bit of discipline but the results and feel good factor make it worthwhile. When the hotel near our home opened a health club, my husband and I were one of the first couples to join. I really enjoy going there and it is very relaxing for me.

Our winters in Scotland are not always conducive to doing any exercise outdoors, so getting over to the club has been a great blessing to me. Perhaps there is a health club near you or maybe even regular keep fit classes. Or maybe your job is a 'work out' in itself! You could take 'Zumba' classes. They are great fun and give you a good workout. You also meet lots of new people, which is always good.

I encourage you to do what you can and ask God to do what you can't.

HRT

Some women opt for Hormone Replacement Therapy, and do well on that. I have got to the 'other side' of the change of life without HRT, but that was my choice. You have to do what you believe is best for you. Talk to your doctor and get advice. Like I said before, there are excellent natural and herbal remedies that are also available for helping with the symptoms of menopause.

Why should you and your family suffer unnecessarily when there is help available? Your relationship with your husband is precious in the sight of God. Don't let the enemy cause division in the home, through you not being able to cope with menopause.

I used to experience hot flushes and night sweats. It felt like I was boiling on the inside! When this would happen, I would pray for God's peace and just let it pass. Cutting down on caffeine and drinking plenty of water does help. In the evenings I drink decaffeinated tea and coffee in moderation.

At night, I would get so hot I would push the duvet cover off me. A few minutes later I would feel the cold and I would pull up the duvet! My poor, long suffering husband was very thankful when I got over that stage. It seems the longer we are married, the bigger the bed we need! When we were first married, we could have shared a single bed and loved it! Then we had a double bed and that was nice.

We then got a king–size bed. Then came menopause and we opted for a super king size bed!! Now there is plenty of space to spread out when I got hot and bothered. At least my husband didn't feel like he was lying beside a heat generator.

We can laugh about it now, but at the time we had to exercise a lot of patience and forbearance towards one another. A sense of humour goes a long way and it helps take the tension out of a potentially volatile situation, when you can laugh and not resort to arguing and shouting!

Vaginal dryness can cause pain during love making, and can make you uncomfortable. There are creams that help so do ask your doctor if you feel you need some lubrication. You may not always feel like love making as the hormone levels are depleting but this can put pressure on the marriage if you keep denying your husband. Open communication is vital and with patience and consideration one for the other, you can come to an agreement, which will help you through what can be a difficult time. You may also feel tenderness in your breasts, so you need to let your husband know so that he is aware of this. Don't use menopause as an excuse to avoid having sex. There are many good books that you can get which will help keep the spark in your marriage alive. No matter how old you are you can enjoy a healthy, satisfying sex life with your husband.

One of the most distressing symptoms that many women battle with during menopause is the terrible mood swings they experience. One minute they feel great, the next minute they feel depressed. Many women struggle with feelings of inadequacy and can't cope with any pressure at all. These mood swings are brought on by the hormonal changes that take place in our bodies. We need to understand that this is a natural part of being a woman and we can get through this.

Pre-menstrual tension, postnatal depression and the hormonal swings that occur in our bodies during pregnancy, are all part of the make up of a woman. Just as we don't have to receive sickness and disease in our bodies and in our minds, so we don't have to receive all the symptoms of menopause!

We can choose to walk in God's word and believe in Him for our healing. I chose to believe God for healing for my body and peace for my mind and I did get to the 'other side' of menopause without undue distress! God will do for you what He did for me. Exercise your faith and ask Him to help you.

I do my best to look good. When you don't feel good about yourself, the tendency is to let yourself go, which makes you feel even worse. Do the best you can to dress nicely, even if you have put on some weight. There are so many lovely styles that can cover and flatter the fuller figure. Believe me when I say I have been there, many times! I am only five foot one, so when I put on weight it shows. I choose loose, comfortable styles, which don't have to be frumpy!

My daughter always keeps me right with fashion. If something looks ridiculous, she tells me.

She told me once not to buy anything she wouldn't wear! She is also very honest with me and I appreciate that. I prefer that to false flattery and I always try to take on board good, constructive advice. Don't get into a rut with your fashion. Decide today you don't do boring! Try a new look and enjoy the 'feel good about yourself' factor. Don't feel guilty about spending money on yourself. Tell yourself you deserve it and enjoy the approval and delight of your husband and family.

I learned to use make up and also how to keep my hair nice without too much bother. When my hair looks nice, I feel good. Having your hair done doesn't have to cost the earth. I have gone to the same hairdresser for years now. She knows what I like and I am not afraid to tell her if I don't like something she is doing to my hair. It is my hair after all, and she needs to know what I am looking for. I like to change my hairstyle every so often and try to have a style that I can manage. Hair colour and texture change with age and the styles that suited me when I was younger just don't work for me now. There are good hair products on the market that can help and if you are going grey, you may have to lighten your natural hair colour. I was a brunette, but since going grey, I am now blonde.

I got set free from feeling guilty about looking after myself. I always thought that everyone else was more deserving than I was and I would always buy for our family first. I still love to bless our children and grandchildren, but I can now enjoy just shopping for me.

I'm liberated, but not frivolous with money, for which my husband is thankful! You can have the time of your life by having a fresh look at the menopause. Don't see it as the end of your sexuality as a woman, but see it as a new season in your life as a woman.

If you have a husband, then start planning how you can enjoy doing things together at this new and exciting time in your life. My sister-in-law is learning how to play golf so she and her husband can do things together. There are many things you can do; new hobbies, sports, books to read, places to go, people to see. Think about all the things you wanted to do when the children were young and that you put off till 'one day'.

Well, that one day can be today!

My husband always says that life is an 'adventure'. It is, if you let it! You just have to get your mind around it.

7 STEPS TO A HAPPIER YOU

1. Live in the Present

Don't waste any more time regretting what's gone before and worrying about what's going to come. Resentment means re-feeling. When you find yourself doing this, bring your attention back to the fact that you are living right now. Living in the present also allows you to be wholly with the people you are with and what you are doing, so you can make the most of it.

2. Don't Try to Change Others

Only God can change a person. Accept that you can only change yourself. Focus on your good points and your strengths, rather than on your weaknesses. Even if you are over forty, it's not too late.

3. Think Happy

Your happiness levels go up and down due to circumstances, but your thoughts are the biggest factor in dictating how you feel. I shared earlier in this chapter that you have to take your thoughts captive. The way we think about something or someone, totally influences how we feel. Tell yourself you're happy and start being thankful, even if there is a mountain of problems in your path. If you are ill, see yourself well and take each day at a time.

4. Don't Live in the Problem – Live in the Solution

Don't think, talk and live with what's wrong. Start thinking on solutions and you will start thinking positively. Confront any difficult situations and work out what would make it better.

5. Take Time to be Grateful

Thank God for all the good things He has blessed you with and for His grace to work through difficult situations. Take the time to be thankful and express your thanks to God and to those around you whenever you get the opportunity.

6. Understand Your Moods

Your moods can be up and down like a yo–yo. Don't get hopeless or helpless. It could be your hormones and it will pass. For some women these shifts are slight, for others, it can be extreme. Don't react or make decisions when you are down, just keep putting one foot in front of the other and you will get through it.

7. Connect With Other People

Be open, and truthful. Love people and allow people to love you. Always remember you are not on your own, you can get help. Call a friend and go out for a coffee. It's good to talk and often a bit of company can take your mind off yourself.

21

The Grandmother

She was so proud of her granddaughter. What a radiant bride she was, her joy emanating from her like a light. Her long, blonde hair was pinned up but already soft, wavy tendrils were falling down. Her new husband gazed upon her in adoration. He had got a prize this day. She prayed that he would always see his new bride in the same way, as a prize, to be cherished and cared for.

Her thoughts took her back to her own wedding day fifty years ago. She was only sixteen when she married Joseph. They didn't have much, except their love and their dreams. That love had taken them through many tough times; when Joseph was out of work, when they buried two children, when she fought breast cancer and when she nursed Joseph after his heart surgery. He had passed away two years ago, just weeks after his 70th birthday. She had watched him fight the tiredness and eventually come to terms with the fact that he had to rest more.

They had worked hard together to realise their dream of owning their own farm and producing their own brand of produce. That had been her idea. Together they had worked late hours preserving fruits and pickles, growing and harvesting fresh fruit and veg. Their brand products were now sold in every big supermarket chain! No more did she stand behind a wooden table set up outside the house. People used to drive for miles to buy their produce.

Expansion, corporations and all the pressure that came with that, she blamed for Joseph's condition. When did the dream take control of their lives and become their master? She didn't have to worry about finances and she was thankful for that. She was well taken care of, but she was so lonely. She missed Joseph so much.

Her two sons lived in different parts of the country and were involved as directors in the business. She saw them at Christmas and Easter. They had always been independent, even as boys. Joseph had insisted on private boarding schooling for them, so they had missed out on the closeness of home. They didn't resent her for that, in fact, they were thankful for the contacts and friends they had made at their school. They were well-educated and could mix with people of any background or culture. Well-travelled, sports enthusiasts, Joseph had financed their every whim.

Not so with her daughter, the beautiful, poised mother of the bride. She and Joseph had agreed she could stay at home and attend the local school. She had all their love lavished on her and she had blossomed in the security of knowing they were there for her. She met and married a local lad when she was twenty, and had settled in a house two streets away from Joseph and herself.

Life had not always been easy for her, but she had always been able to come and share her problems with her mother. Openness and honesty is something she always emphasised, but more importantly, having God at the centre of the home and taking everything to Him in prayer. She blamed herself for the lack of faith in her sons life. She had neglected the most important education of all, the knowledge of God. She had thought the school would teach them and guide them, but all they had was religion – a form of Godliness, but with no relationship with Jesus. Not so with her daughter. She had been brought up in the local church and her faith was a way of life to her and her family. And now her Granddaughter stood at the altar in the church where she herself had been married.

Full Circle!

She heard that familiar quiet voice on the inside of her. "Be thankful, be at peace, don't look back, you still have so much to impart, it's not over for you, not yet. There are people to see and speak to, people that don't know Me. Pray for your sons, ask of Me and trust Me… You have wisdom to impart. Be thankful".

She closed her eyes and smiled. All would be well. The God who brought her through the hard times had not changed. He would do the same for her family.

The ceremony was over. They were now married. As the new bride and groom walked down the aisle, her granddaughter stopped and looked at her. "Oh Gran, thank you for everything."

She was thankful.

22

Being a Wise Grandmother

While out walking early one morning, the path I was walking on was rough, but straight. Because I knew it well, I knew where not to step!

Just like grandmothers...

They have travelled paths and can give advice and direction, wisdom and experience. They can direct you down paths and help you to avoid the stumbling blocks and pitfalls of life. We all like to take the easy and shortest routes, but sometimes shortcuts are not the best route! Life is a journey, and we have to make sure we are on the right track.

Because of the breakdown of family values and the changes in society, grandparents can play an important role in stabilizing the lives of their grandchildren. We are carriers of culture and tradition from one generation to the next, connecting links that can keep our families rooted in good core values. We have the opportunity to pass on wisdom and more importantly, we can serve as a spiritual catalyst to the younger generation, demonstrating for them the reality of life in Christ.

I always share the goodness of God with our grandchildren. When we celebrated our 40th wedding anniversary it had always been our dream to take our whole family to Florida. We booked the air tickets and a villa and enjoyed two weeks of fun and laughter. We made so many memories. You cannot leave this earth without making memories. In the midst of having the family around us, we shared with them how it was the provision of God that enabled us to take them on this special trip.

Bernie and I make sure we make time for our grandchildren. Yes, we do have a lot on and it would be easy to get caught up in the works of the ministry to the extent that everything else gets neglected. Our grandchildren are important to us and we communicate that to them, by making time for them. The result is that they know they are loved and valued and they also understand that we do have commitments to our church but they don't resent that. Let your family know they come first, by showing them that through your actions. Bernie regularly takes our grandsons out for the day. They have a great time and he loves it. We take the girls out too and spoil them. These times together are precious and we get the opportunity to tell of our love for God, all that He is and all He has done for us. We explain to them why we worship God and attend church. We tell them of God's healing, provision and protection and of answered prayer. Our heart is to see our children's children serving God and being a witness to all. When you neglect your family, they will end up resenting God and church and that is the reason many backslide and turn to other things. My grandchildren keep me young at heart, in mind and body, and bring me great joy for which I am most thankful.

Young people need stability and a sense of their own past, as well as a hope for the future. They need what we can give them, the reality of the faithfulness of God. We can give them security, acceptance, time and love. We can be a support to our children as they attempt the demanding task of parenting. Grand–parenting is such a wonderful and rewarding time for women. All the mistakes I made with my children need never be repeated. I have more time and patience for my grandchildren and love them so much. I enjoy their visits and share in babysitting when I can.

Many women find themselves having to look after their grandchildren full time because the parents are working. Now that is fine if you have no problems with that and are fit and healthy, but there are women who do this through a feeling of guilt and put their lives on hold. If you find yourself in that position, you need to balance out the time you spend babysitting and the time you need for yourself. It is not wrong to say no sometimes. Remember, you live life by choice and not by chance.

As a grandmother, I do not interfere in the parenting and disciplining of our grandchildren. I do my best to adhere to the boundaries the parents have laid down. I do admit to spoiling them a wee bit and they know that Granny always has goodies for them and a place where they can come and just chill out. When all our grandchildren get together it can be a bit noisy but we all have a great time together. We can unite our family. I have always encouraged our children to get together and regularly host them all in our home. Christmas, Easter, birthdays, anniversaries are all a time of family celebration. Even the most cynical and jaded young person can be brought back to family values in the midst of family traditions.

It is sad when families become fragmented and out of touch. Relationships are built by making time to be with one another. I don't want to end my life lonely and self centred. I want to be surrounded by family and friends who know me and love me for who I am. That is true riches. When someone dies you never hear him or her say they regretted not having spent more time at work! Their biggest regret is that they didn't make time for their family. My husband has a saying that goes like this, "Spend more time in making a life, than on making a living!" Children grow up so quickly, so take every opportunity to be with them and invest in their lives.

If you have children who have divorced, you can be the safe haven for the grandchildren. Don't take sides or point the finger but just be there for them and let them know that there is security and stability in your home and that they will always be a part of your life.

Many less than ideal situations begin with sadness, but can have a happy outcome when we help them through the transition of divorce or bereavement. Many grandchildren come to their grandparents confused and hurt, often filled with anger, resentment and guilt they don't understand. A grandmother can provide a fair and objective listening ear and a place of security and love. It helps them because you are not caught up in the problem and you can help them work through the sense of loss they feel.

As grandparents who love and follow Christ, we can give our grandchildren a pattern of righteousness that will help them be strong enough to stand no matter what they face in life. We invest in the spiritual growth of our grandchildren and teach them honour in the home and to honour God. We tell them of the goodness of God and how much He loves them and has a great plan for their lives. We live the life of faith before them and by our example they can see that God is true to His word and He answers prayer. They are not embarrassed to pray aloud or talk of their faith openly. It is their habit to pray over their food and to be thankful for God's blessings in their lives.

We have shown them never to be ashamed of their love for God and His word. If we want to see the future of the church established in our nations then we have to invest in our grandchildren. They are our future.

We can always find common ground with young people. I get my grandchildren to help me with any technical equipment in my home, like computers, TV, etc. I never cease to be amazed at how easy it is for them to figure out what can take me hours! I ask them about the music, films and books they are into, and I like to meet their friends. Not all the music they listen to is awful and loud, and not all their friends are weird! Never judge young people by how they look. If you do, you are missing out on a great and wonderful part of your life. My grandchildren help keep me having a youthful and positive outlook on life, and I get much joy from them.

We are here to provide support by encouraging communication and openness in our families. Enjoy the time with them, for they too will grow up and then you will be a Great grandmother!!

23

Death of a Loved One

They had decided they would each share their own special memories of Mum. It was time now for the letters to be read out to all who had come to Mum's memorial service. The eldest would begin with her letter.

Dear Mum,

We will miss you. You were always the centre of our family, cooking, serving, taking care of the grandchildren, so we could eat and catch up with one another. It was important to you that we stayed close as a family. You will be with Dad now and you wouldn't trade places with the living, not for anything.

Thank you Mum for the values and traditions you gave us, a rich heritage, which will endure for future generations. As the eldest daughter, I commit to keeping the same values and traditions and to pass them onto your grandchildren.

I'm going to miss you. We all will, but today's not a day to be sad. It's a day to say goodbye and be thankful that you are now with Jesus. We want you to know we love you.

Goodbye Mum.

Dear Mum,

You were not the type of person who loved us based on how well we performed. You always loved us equally and accepted us, warts and all. You were always telling us we were a work in progress and not to be discouraged because God wasn't finished with us yet.

When I was younger I rebelled against your wisdom and counsel, but now I have children of my own, I can look back and see just how wise you were. The older I got, the wiser you got!

You helped me through many difficult times. You were my constant in a life full of change. Dad would say that change was here to stay. Everything changed when he died, but you were the one who comforted us and helped us through the grieving process. Now you're with him and all those loved ones who have gone before you.

Thank you Mum for the example you set us and for the love you gave us. Thank you for your prayers and your faith, which never wavered.

I missed out on family outings and holidays because I distanced myself from you all. I was rebellious and blamed the family, God and everybody else, for all the stuff I was going through. During that time you and Dad never stopped praying for me and you never gave up on me, even when I gave up on myself. You believed in me and knew I would find the path that led back to home and to God.

He smiled, unashamed of the tears running down his face.

There are so many great memories I could share today. The holidays, the funny things and the difficult times we went through as a family.

But I want to remember how much you loved me when I was unlovable.

Now you are gone but we, your children, have the legacy of the love you left behind.

Thank you. I will miss you, but will see you when it is my time to be with Jesus.

Dear Mum,

You were exactly who you needed to be for each of us. As your daughter, you were always there to help me with the children. When we shopped, you would look after them so I could try on clothes in the changing rooms. You always asked and valued my opinion before you made a purchase. You wanted to be chic without being gross. "Don't wear anything I wouldn't wear Mum."

I would tell you when you had lipstick on your teeth and if certain outfits were too young for you. I'm going to miss those times.

When I went through a time of insecurity you were the one who affirmed me and encouraged me to stretch myself. I can still hear your words, "You serve a limitless God, so don't limit yourself".

Mum, you and Dad were interested in people and right now you'll be rejoicing with the saints in heaven, catching up with all the friends who went before you.

Thank you for the love and support you gave me. Thank you for your input into my life. You taught me that my husband and children are the most important people in my life and how to be a good wife and mother.

She closed her eyes.

You were the best. I'll always love you Mum. Goodbye and I'll do my best to stay sweet.

Her husband joined her.

Dear Mum,

You were a great mother-in-law and I'm thankful for your wisdom and input into our lives.

Goodbye.

As he stood by her side, she lowered her head and let out a small sob, but quickly she looked out to the precious faces of family, friends and church members. A tear rolled down her cheek as she smiled at them.

"Mum loved every one of you and it means so much to us that you are here celebrating her homecoming. Thank you."

Her daughter–in–law summed up her life by reading Proverbs chapter 31.

The pastor of the church shared the eulogy.

She was a woman who lived life to the full. She loved her family and friends and she loved this church. Her love for God was the motivation for all she did and she will be sorely missed.

We would all do well to follow her example. When you think of her, remember her love, joy and peace.

She would not have wanted me to close this service without giving everyone here today an invitation to embrace the peace and joy she knew. Her life was encapsulated in one person, Jesus Christ, her beloved Lord and Saviour.

You too can have a relationship with Him, by inviting Him to come into your heart and confessing Him as your Lord and Saviour. Tell Him you are sorry for your sins and He will forgive you and wash you clean. You get a fresh start in life and the opportunity to serve God and know Him as your loving Father".

There were some who responded to the invitation that day and had their lives changed irrevocably. That would have given Mum the greatest joy of all, that even in death, there is life.

1 Corinthians 15:55

Oh death, where is your victory? Oh death, where is your sting?

24

Dealing with Death

The subject of death is not one we like to deal with. Education prepares us for work, marriage, parenthood and life, but I have never heard of schools that have classes on preparing us for death! The horror of death is universal, yet death is a part of life. Surprisingly, one of the two events common to every human being's existence has been considered as unnatural by every generation of man, including our own. Why is that? I believe it is because we cannot explain it's mystery and the unknown makes us fearful. But we cannot live in denial. When you accept the fact of death, it frees you to live!

Contained in the Psalms, David made these statements.

Psalm 90:12

Lord, let me know my end, and what is the measure of my days. Let me know how fleeting my life is. You have made my days a few handbreadths, and my lifetime is as nothing in Your sight. Surely, every man goes about as a shadow. Surely for nothing are they in turmoil; man heaps up, and knows not who will gather...

Revised Standard Version

So teach us to number our days that we may get a heart of wisdom.

Death can overtake us in many ways; disease, war, accidents, diet, stress or simply your body wearing out. When a loved one dies of old age it is easier to accept, but premature death is always difficult and brings with it many questions.

In 2001 my brother–in–law lost his wife and four-year–old daughter in a fire. He nearly lost his life trying to save them and still has scarring to his lungs, which thankfully, is treatable. When he was released from the hospital after five weeks, he came and lived with my husband and I for the next eight months. This was a very difficult time for him and the family, the funeral being particularly hard. By God's grace we all got through the loss and the grief. I cannot think how anyone can come through a situation like this without faith in God. Today, my brother–in–law has remarried and has made his peace with God. He is an inspiration to all who meet him, and a testimony to the healing power of God in his life. Through observing how he coped with his loss, I learned so much.

As a minister, I had to learn how to help people through the loss of a loved one and one of the hardest things to bear is the death of a child. I don't have all the answers, nor do I think anyone has, but I do know that we can be a comfort to people and help them through their loss.

Managing Grief

Death is like a wound to the living. Everyone we know who dies has an effect on us. I have friends who have lost a husband and it takes time for them to heal. When people are grieving they have to deal with so many emotions. One of these is guilt and regret. They always feel they didn't spend enough time with the person or they had things they left unsaid. They feel anger towards the one who died for leaving them. Some people get angry with God and blame Him for everything that went wrong or simply for the death. These responses to death are normal, or at least normal for a person who deeply loved the one who died, and with time, they will wear off. It could be said that any natural response to death is normal, but any unnatural one may delay the healing process and be potentially dangerous.

What is a natural response to death?

My answer would be grief and tears, an overwhelming sense of loss and the desire to be alone. For some it could be to question God's wisdom and even His love. This sort of questioning does not turn God away from us, but brings Him closer to us. The Holy Spirit can then be to us, the Comforter and Friend He is.

Another natural response to death is to idealize the one who died. Often guilt can make the person larger than life size in our memory.

Another response is found in the way people feel bound to the one who died. "What would he/she want me to do?" "How can I carry on their work?" These are not unusual reactions to grief.

Exposure to death creates in some, a fear of their own death. This was the case for me when my brother died at the age of twenty–one. Until then, I had never thought about death or dying, but I found myself dwelling on death. This opened me up to the fear of death. I only overcame this fear when I became a Christian in 1979, while living in South Africa.

I believe all fear is rooted in the fear of death. This can only be overcome through committing one's life to Christ and being born again. Our Saviour, Jesus, becomes our peace when He lives within us.

Unnatural grief is toxic and has to be overcome. Guilt is also difficult to overcome. Death closes the door on making things right and opens the door to a flood of "If only…." thoughts. Make the decision not to go down that route. It is a path that leads to depression. Get help if you need to, but choose to move away from regret and guilt.

Life must move forward, even though we may have lost the one who was dearest to us, even though meaning seems to have been removed from living. If we feel guilty, we must receive forgiveness. The solution to self–pity is to feel pity for someone else and move in the direction of holding that person up. If you have worked through grief, then you can help someone else do the same. This sort of emotional investment is a large part of the healing we need for death's wound. When I feel down or sorry for myself, my cure is to get around people and be a blessing to them. It takes me 'out of myself!'

In the healing process we will find that the memory of the person who died is freed from sickbed and coffin, to recall the person he/she really was: laughing, encouraging, working, playing, loving and life size.

I pray the comfort of the Holy Spirit and the love of God will help you through your loss.

The Hard Questions on Death

All of us in our lifetime will experience the death of a family member or friend. Every one of us will face death. At this very moment as I write this chapter I am moving towards the end of my life! I am not being morbid, but the truth is our body is decaying daily!

Now, there are a lot of things we can do to put that off, like diet, exercise, thought life and the like. But no matter how well we take care of our body, we will die one day. My question to you is, are you prepared for death? How do you deal with the death of a loved one?

I was asked to share with the second year pupils in a local high school, on the subject of what a Christian believes on life after death. I have been doing this on an annual basis for many years now. After every session I take questions and have found that every class asks the same questions. In over thirty years of ministry when dealing with the subject of death, everyone asks the same questions. From thirteen and on, the questions are the same.

* Is there a Heaven?
* What is it like?
* Is Hell real?
* Is there such a thing as a ghost?
* What about reincarnation?

But the big question remains the same, is there life after death?

The Withered Leaf

All mankind is of one author, and is one volume; when one man dies, one chapter is not torn out of the book, but translated into a better language; and every chapter must be so translated. God employs several translators; some by age, some by sickness, some by war, some by justice; but God's hand is in every translation; and His hand shall bind up all our scattered leaves again, for that library, where every book shall lie open to one another.

John Donne (1573 – 1631)

Young or old, today you are living life, loving and being loved by others. You may be hurting or maybe you have hurt others. Just like the cold wind tears the leaves from the branches, we too, like a leaf, fall to the ground and mingle with the dust. From dust we came and from dust we return. I love the smell of autumn. That woody, musky smell, fresh yet pungent. Is life like a leaf that falls and decays, or is there something beyond the grave?

Christians believe that there is life after death and that Jesus Christ Himself died and rose again. They also believe that He will bring to life again all those who believe in Him. There are countless millions of souls who are longing for light, truth and life. Souls are looking for answers. This is the reason so many people are interested in the occult and in the supernatural. They will go to a spiritualist meeting to try and contact their lost loved one.

Has anyone died and come back to tell us of life after death? Is there a Heaven to be gained and a Hell to be shunned? If they have, how can they prove it? We want evidence, hard facts! We want something we can touch, hear, see, smell or taste!

Just like Thomas, the disciple who doubted that Jesus had risen from the dead, we want to see the nails marks and put our fingers in.

John 20:24–29 (Message Bible)

But Thomas, sometimes called the Twin, one of the Twelve, was not with them when Jesus came. The other disciples told him, "We saw the Master."

But he said, "Unless I see the nail holes in His hands, put my finger in the nail holes, and stick my hand in His side, I won't believe it."

Eight days later, his disciples were again in the room. This time Thomas was with them. Jesus came through the locked doors, stood among them, and said, "Peace to you."

Then He focused His attention on Thomas. "Take your finger and examine My hands. Take your hand and stick it in My side. Don't be unbelieving, believe".

Thomas said, "My Master! My God."

Jesus said, "So, you believe because you've seen with your own eyes. Even better blessings are in store for those who believe without seeing."

Everything a Christian believes is based on the bible, God's Word to us. His word brings light, life and truth. God's word on Heaven and Hell are to be found in the bible. If you want to know what Heaven is like, go to the scriptures that describe it. I have not seen Jesus with my physical eyes, but I believe He is the Son of God who died on the cross and gave His life for me and for you. My hard evidence for that is found in many scriptures throughout the Old and New Testaments. I have faith in the written Word of God.

Hebrews 11:1 (New King James Version)

Now faith is the substance of things hoped for, the evidence of things not seen.

Authentic Version

Now faith forms a solid ground for expectations, the proof of unseen realities.

New English Bible

And what is faith? Faith gives substance to our hopes, and makes us certain of realities we do not see.

Jordan Version

Faith is betting your life on the unseen!

Just because we have never seen or experienced things before, does not mean they don't exist, or that we should fear them.

A little boy wrote a letter to God, addressed it to heaven and mailed it. Letters like that usually end up in the dead letter office, but somehow this one was opened. It read;

> *Dear God,*
>
> *What's it like to die? I don't want to do it, I just want to know.*
>
> *Your friend,*
>
> *Bobby.*

It's a question all have pondered.

Harold Sala writes: "When I'm going to a part of the world I have never been to, I read and investigate to find out what it's like. I browse travel books, go on the Internet, and talk with someone who can tell me what it's like from personal experience. No other book in the world can tell me what the Bible tells me about Heaven. The only person who has been there and can tell me what it's like is Jesus."

Knowing that for the believer, death is just a transition into God's presence, Paul the apostle writes: *"When these bodies are destroyed, God will give us a place to live in Heaven." 2 Corinthians 5:1 (Contemporary English Version)*

I like to think on dying as just changing location without having to pack your bags!

At the end of C.S. Lewis's book, *'The Last Battle'*, the characters die in a train accident, and C.S. Lewis concludes the story like this: The things that happened after that were so beautiful I cannot write them. For us this is the end of all stories, but for them it was only the beginning of the real story.

Speaking about Heaven Paul says, *"If I had to choose right now, I hardly know which to choose. The desire to break camp here and be with Christ is powerful. Some days I can think of nothing better." Philippians 1:22 (Message Bible)*

Hell

For the believer who has their faith in Christ and the assurance of an eternity with Him in Heaven, there is no fear of death. But what about those who don't have that affirmation, or who wilfully will not commit to Christ? Will they go to Hell? The bible says they will, but we cannot know where individuals will spend eternity, for only God knows a man's heart. It is not for us to judge people, but rather to pray for them and use every opportunity to share with them the Gospel message. However, regarding Hell, the bible has many scriptures, which confirm that Hell is a real location to be avoided at all costs.

In 2011 I attended a conference where one of the speakers was a man called Bill Weise. I had never heard of him before this and I had the pleasure of meeting him and his wife after the service. He has written a book entitled '23 *Minutes In Hell*', and he shared at the conference from the book. God allowed him to experience the horrors of Hell and instructed him to tell people about Hell's reality. What impacted me most were the scriptures he shared to back up everything that God allowed him to see and experience.

You may question a person's experience, but we cannot question God's Word, which is truth. His very graphic description of the torment and suffering in Hell increased my resolve to share the Gospel at every opportunity.

Hell is real and contrary to some people's beliefs; it is not in our suffering here on earth that we experience Hell. It is much worse than all we can ever imagine. If you don't have the assurance of an eternity in heaven, then don't delay and ask Jesus into your life as Lord and Saviour and give your life to Him. You will experience the peace and joy that can only be found in Him.

Heaven

The bible describes Heaven as a place of light and life filled with the glory of God. It is a place vibrating with worship and music, a place of harmony. There is no sickness or suffering there. *Revelation chapters 21* and *22* reveal a place of beauty, where the streets are paved with gold, the walls are made of precious stones and the gates are solid pearl. I encourage you to seek out and study all the scriptures on Heaven.

The life we live on earth is temporary and will cease when we die. But the real you, the person on the inside who is spirit, will never die. I know people who have had a 'death bed' conversion and I thank God they made their peace with Him before it was too late. But, that is not the best God has for us. He wants us to live in His abundance, exercising our authority here and now, on earth. Our time here on earth determines our status in eternity. It is here we can choose to come to Jesus and find our purpose and seal our eternity. By doing nothing, we choose by default! It is here on earth where we develop and grow in our relationship with God. When we get to heaven we will stand close to Jesus. When we worship God, His presence is with us, angels are present, and we connect with God. Worship is one of the things we will be familiar with in Heaven. That is why we need to learn how to worship God in spirit and in truth. God is looking for worshippers and our worship will carry through into eternity. As a Christian, Heaven is our destination.

Colossians 3:1–4

If then you have been raised with Christ to a new life, thus sharing His resurrection from the dead, aim at and seek the rich eternal treasures that are above, where Christ is seated at the right hand of God.

And set your minds and keep them set on what is above, the higher things, not on things that are on the earth.

For as far as this world is concerned you have died, and your new real life is hidden with Christ in God.

When Christ, Who is our life, appears, then you also will appear with Him in the splendour of His glory.

2 Corinthians 5:6–9

So we are always confident, knowing that while we are at home in the body we are absent from the Lord. For we walk by faith, not by sight. We are confident, yes, well pleased rather to be absent from the body and to be present with the Lord. Therefore we make it our aim, whether present or absent, to be well pleasing to Him.

"If I ever reach heaven I expect to find three wonders there: first, to meet some I had not thought to see there; second, to miss some I had expected to see there; and third, the greatest wonder of all, to find myself there"

Anon

John 3:16

For God so loved the world that He gave His only Son, that whoever believes on Him would not perish, but have eternal life.

Ephesians 2:8

For by grace you have been saved through faith, and that not of yourselves, it is the gift of God.

Romans 10:8–10

But what does it say? The word is near you, even in your mouth and in your heart, that is the word of faith, which we preach. That if you confess with your mouth the Lord Jesus and believe in your heart that God has raised Him from the dead, you will be saved. For with the heart one believes to righteousness, and with the mouth confession is made to salvation.

A prayer from the heart, spoken with the mouth in all sincerity, will bring you into a new life in Christ Jesus and secure your place in heaven. If you have never done this, and want to, I would be remiss, if I did not give you the opportunity to do so now.

Pray this out loud,

Dear God,

I want to be the woman you created me to be and live out Your purpose for my life. I'm sorry for all the wrongs I have done and repent of all my sin and ask You to forgive me. I do believe that Jesus Christ died on the cross for me and He rose again from the dead on the third day. I ask Him into my life as my Lord and Saviour. I receive Your forgiveness and I thank You for the blood of Jesus, which washes me from all sin.

I am born again, a new creation in Christ. I thank You, that old things are passed away, and all things have become brand new. I thank you Father, that I am now your daughter, and I will serve you and honour You all the days of my life through to eternity.

In Jesus name I pray,

Amen

You have just embarked on the most exciting and rewarding phase in your life.

May God bless you and keep you.

May His face shine upon you, and may you walk in His peace all the days of your life.

Amen.

25

Living to a Ripe Old Age

I believe that we should aim to live long and to end our life with dignity and strength. God promises us 120 years by reason of strength. You may not want to be around that long, but you can determine to have the best life, by making the right choices now.

I believe we have to pay the price to live longer and stronger. We do this by taking care of our bodies, like sticking to a healthy diet, exercising, taking supplements and using wisdom when it comes to over working and the likes.

I am not going to go into any of these in depth in this book, as there are plenty of good books on nutrition and healthy lifestyle that we can read. I want rather, to focus in on the mindset we need in order to live long. The first thing we need to do is set our sights on living long. As with everything in life, there is direction to be found in the word of God.

When I read the scriptures on God's promises for a full and abundant life, I then have a responsibility to take them and start declaring them. I need to develop my faith in whatever area I want to see change.

You cannot talk sickness and disease and think that you will be healed. You cannot talk lack and fear and think you will have all your needs met. You cannot talk old age and think you will live to a hundred.

To live to a ripe old age, you must learn to live by faith, and that means believing and declaring God's word and acting on it every day. You will have to see yourself living long, seeing your grandchildren married and being present at your great–grandchildren's dedication service.

Psalm 103:2–5 (New King James Version)

Bless the Lord Oh my soul, and forget not all His benefits, who forgives all your iniquities, who heals all your diseases, who redeems your life from destruction, who crowns you with loving kindness and tender mercies, who satisfies your mouth with good things wo that your youth is renewed like the eagle's.

Psalm 92:13,14 (Amplified Bible)

Planted in the house of the Lord, they shall flourish in the courts of our God.

Growing in grace, they shall still bring forth fruit in old age; they shall be full of sap, spiritual vitality and rich in the verdure of love, trust and contentment.

Isaiah 40:31 (New King James Version)

They that wait upon the Lord shall renew their strength, they shall mount up with wings as eagles, they shall run and not be weary, and they shall walk and shall not faint.

I want to live the latter part of my life with vitality and I still want to reach out to people and make a difference to them for their good. I want to leave a legacy to my children and to their children that will cause them to stand strong and take them through whatever they have to face in their lifetime.

Who knows what the world will be like in years to come? It would seem that wickedness and apostasy is on the increase, but we know that God will never fail us, and those who trust in God will overcome regardless of circumstances. I see a generation rising up, full of faith and passionate for the cause of Christ. That is the legacy I want to leave, especially here in the nation of Scotland.

I don't know the day or the hour when my spirit will depart from my body, but from now until that day comes, I want to live the best life I can and touch as many lives as I can. I want to be like the apostle Paul, who said he had finished his course and run his race. It's not over till it's over!

Psalm 118:17

I shall not die, but live, and declare the works of the Lord.

Psalm 103:4 (New Living Translation)

God ransoms me from death and surrounds me with love and tender mercies

Psalm 116:8–9 (Amplified Bible)

He has delivered my life from death, my eyes from tears, and my feet from stumbling and falling. I will walk before the Lord in the land of the living.

Psalm 121:7–8 (Amplified Bible)

The Lord will keep me from all evil, He will keep my life. The Lord will keep my going out and my coming in from this time forth and forevermore.

Psalm 91:16 (Amplified Bible)

With long life will I satisfy him, and show him My salvation.

26

Missed Opportunities

2 Timothy 4:6–7 (Message Bible)

You take over. I'm about to die, my life an offering on God's alter. This is the only race with running. I've run hard right to the finish, believed all the way.

As the apostle Paul prepared to die, he is in the process of coming to terms with every person who had a problem with him. "Bring Mark, come before winter." Paul, before he goes home to be with Jesus, wants to tie up all the loose ends! He reveals his heart. There is no bitterness, no resentment, but he is determined to deal with the people around him before he dies.

Old age is a time of introspection and looking back on life. We all want to live to a ripe old age but there are no guarantees. We need to make right with family members and friends, before we die and remove any misunderstandings and make peace with them.

Whether they die first, or you do, don't wait till the funeral! To give somebody tribute over his or her coffin is too late. How many of us have missed an opportunity to tell others how much we appreciate and love them?

I regret that I didn't tell my own mum and dad more often, that I loved and appreciated them, and thanked them for all they did for me. My dad passed away very suddenly in 2001 and I didn't get to the hospital in time to be with him in his last moments. Without going into too much detail, it turned out I could have been with him, had the communication from the hospital been better. I deeply regret this but have had to come to terms with it and move on.

Perhaps an illness or accident has snatched a loved one away before you had the chance to express your love, or put to right a wrong. Pick up the phone or write to them or, if possible go and visit them.

Written on the back of a sugar packet in a restaurant in America: *We more often regret the things that we didn't do than the things we did.*

Lord Balfour states, *"The best thing to give your enemy is forgiveness; to an opponent, tolerance; to a friend, your heart; to your child, a good example; to your father, deference; to your mother, conduct that will make her proud of you; to yourself, respect; to all men, charity."*

Don't take the people around you for granted. Learn to value them and do your best to make everyone you can feel special.

Share the Gospel While You Can

2 Timothy 4:2 (Amplified Bible)

Herald and preach the word! Keep your sense of urgency (stand by and be ready), whether the opportunity seems to be favorable or unfavorable, (Whether it is convenient or inconvenient, whether it is welcome or unwelcome, you as a preacher of the Word are to show people in what way their lives are wrong) And convince them, rebuking and correcting, warning and urging and encouraging them, being unflagging and inexhaustible in patience and teaching.

Now I know the above scripture was written to Timothy who was a young pastor, but I believe that we can all take that scripture to heart and use every opportunity we can to share the Gospel message. I don't believe in 'bible thumping' and pressure, but if we ask God, He will create the time and place so that we can speak to family and friends.

2 Corinthians 5:18

Now all things are of God, who has reconciled us to Himself through Jesus Christ, and has given us the ministry of reconciliation.

I take so much joy in seeing people come to Christ, especially when I have the privilege of sharing the Gospel with them. It was a woman, Mary, who was the first evangelist. She went to the tomb and found the stone rolled away and she ran back to tell the disciples that Jesus was alive.

A soul saved is the most lasting inheritance you can leave. The only thing you can take to heaven with you is people.

Epilogue

Redeemed

She picked herself up from the ground where the Pharisees had thrown her and looked for the first time into the face of the Rabbi. He was still bent down from when he had been writing in the sand. He stood up and looked into her face. She had never seen such love or compassion in the eyes of any man before. All she had ever seen was lust and contempt.

He said "Woman, where are your accusers? Has no man condemned you?" She answered, "No one, Lord!" And Jesus said, "I do not condemn you either. Go your way from now on and sin no more."

She turned away from Him and from the life of sin, guilt and shame. In her heart she decided she would embrace this new life of love, forgiveness, peace and joy.

She would be a follower of the Rabbi and she would serve Him all His days. She had been redeemed as a woman.

She felt worthy for the first time in her life, valuable and precious.

God had judged Eve in the garden when she was deceived and sinned against Him. But He had also given her the promise of One who would come and bruise the serpent's head. He had come and she knew that women everywhere, in every generation, would take their place as God has ordained and they would be fruitful. Transformed from death into life.

The cycle was now complete.

From birth to death we transition the different seasons and phases of our life as a woman. We bring life into this world through the miracle of birth. We nurture our children and do the best we can to leave a legacy that will help them and future generations to live a better life than we did.

But there is no greater legacy than imparting to them that there is a God Who loves them and that they were born on purpose, for a purpose.

We are fearfully and wonderfully made.

This we must never forget.

Nan

Acknowledgements

To my family who gave me much of the content of this book, through life experience.

To our church in Ayrshire who love and support me.

To Samantha Wallace for all her help and encouragement

To Loulita Gill for all her help and advice.

To my wonderful daughter Denise, just because she inspires me and keeps me young.

To all my friends, I love and value you so much.

About the Author

Nan McLaughlin was born in Ayrshire, Scotland, where she met and married her sweetheart Bernie in 1967.

They immigrated to South Africa in 1975 with their three children. It was there in 1979 that Nan became a Christian.

In 1980, they pioneered a church and they have been committed to ministry since then.

Nan helped her husband run a successful business for many years while bringing up the children and being involved in ministry.

God called them back to Scotland and in 1987 they returned and pioneered a church in Kilwinning, Ayrshire.

They pastor The Bridge Church in Irvine and are starting branch churches in various towns in Scotland and in other nations.

All three children and their grandchildren are serving God and work with them at The Bridge.

Bernie has a Men's Ministry called Repairers of the Breach, where he fathers and mentors men to take their place in the home, workplace and community.

Nan assists her husband in the ministry and has a vision to see women everywhere take their place in the church. She teaches faith for daily living in a very practical way and she has a heart to see the church increase in worship and in evangelism.

After many years of teaching and inputting locally in the church, she has moved into speaking in other nations as God leads.

Woman in Transition is her first book and she and Bernie are currently writing a book on healing for every part of the body, a book on pioneering churches in Europe and a book on the gifts and operations of the Holy Spirit.